NEVER SAY CAN'T

How Never Saying "I Can't" Can Lead to Success

By

Frederick L. Brueck

Dear Joanne
With Best wishes,

Frederick L Brueck

Fred

ISBN: 1-4140-0158-4 (e-book)
ISBN: 1-4140-0157-6 (Paperback)

This book is printed on acid free paper.

1stBooks - rev. 12/13/03

CONTENTS

Introduction.. v

The Family.. 1

The Early Years 11

The Farm.. 21

Terrorism In The School.. 27

Boyhood Friends.. 31

The High School Years.. 37

Summer Jobs... 41

Little Man On The Big Campus 47

Dogs, Planes, Guns And Alcohol 55

Living In The Box 61

My First Professional Job 65

My First Farm Visits... 73

Traveling Cheaply 77

Back To School.. 81

The Near Death Experience.. 83

Specialization.. 87

The Frustrations Of Building A House............................... 91

The Scholarship Tour 99

Listen To Your Doctor — Kick The Habit.......................... 103

The Hardest Decision Of My Life 105

Cats And The Visit 107

Cleaning Up The Mess 111

Behind The Iron Curtain 115

The Sheriff Cometh... 123

Flying High 125

Watch Your Step.. 133

The Second Time Around....................................... 137

Traveling Around The World 139

The Thrill Of A Lifetime 151

The Challenges Of Building A Barn.......................... 161

The Good Shepherd 165

The Tornado.. 173

Retirement: Good Or Bad? 181

Another Crisis 189

Lands Of Fire And Ice 193

Dangerous Occupations 201

Life Goes On.. 211

The Final Word 215

INTRODUCTION

This book is an account of one person's life. As you read through the chapters, you may doubt that this is an autobiography. It reads more like a novel. At times it reads like a humorous novel. Some chapters are sad. At other times it reads like a travelogue, visiting exotic foreign countries. Some chapters are learning experiences that might give you some ideas that might help you solve a problem in your life, or they might educate you about something you never knew before. I guarantee you that everything you read is true.

My goal is to encourage you and others, that despite hardship, discouragement, and all the trials of life, you can succeed.

I will use many personal examples of the challenges throughout my life, from childhood to the present.

This book is not all about gloom and doom or my failures and successes. Many of the chapters describe some of the exciting experiences I have had. You will learn about one of the most beautiful and fascinating places on earth via my two trips to Kenya, Africa. I will also take you to the British Isles, Costa Rica, Iceland, Sweden and Denmark, Austria, and the Soviet Union. You will laugh when you read how I overcame the fear of flying by taking flying lessons and eventually became a private pilot. You will read about the hilarity of my attempt to play golf, tennis and learn ballroom dancing. You will find out how I survived a near death experience.

The bottom line of this book is, as my father used to say to me, "There's no such word as 'can't.'" You can and will succeed in life. Never give up. Just keep trying. The intent of this book is to show you how I became successful through the many examples of my life experiences. Perhaps you just might be able to do the same by learning from this book.

ACKNOWLEDGEMENTS

Karen Brueck for typing the Manuscript.

Leslie Deleski for her inspiration.

Erik Hage for reviewing the Manuscript.

CHAPTER 1

THE FAMILY

If anyone had ever told me that someday I would write a book, I would tell them they better have their head examined.

English was my worst subject from grammar school through college. I do not remember ever turning in a book report. But I feel I have something to say that might help you and others get through the pitfalls of life.

This book documents, through many examples, how I learned, through will and determination, to turn a life filled with hardship, discouragement, insecurity and numerous failures, eventually into a successful career. I believe I just might be able to help you turn some problems you might have into opportunities through the many true examples I use throughout this book. All these examples are from my life experiences, some of which were very good and some very bad.

Mom's favorite saying was "Life's a bitch and then you die."

Pops favorite saying was "There's no such word as 'can't.'"

I guess they were both correct, as you will find out later on. I believe that part of my determination to be successful is genetics, so I want to introduce you to my family.

Frederick L. Brueck

Fred C. Brueck Succumbs at 80; Expert on Optics

An expert in minerals with optical qualities, Fred C. Brueck, a Bausch & Lomb Optical Company employe for 65 years, died yesterday (July 27. 1953). He was 80.

Born in Germany, Mr. Brueck came here at the age of 15. He made the trip alone and came directly to Rochester where he had an uncle. From then on, Mr. Brueck worked in various local optical plants.

At Bausch & Lomb, where be was a member of the Early Settlers Club, he did precision work in optics. He also made trips to New York City to purchase quartz crystal for his firm.

T. M. BRUECK, FIRM LEADER, PASSES AT 74

Camera Shutters Credited to His Invention

Theodore M. Brueck, 74, of 260 Mt. Vernon inventor and superintendent of the Ilex Optical Company, which he helped found died yesterday (Oct. 3, 1944).

Mr. Brueck, a native of Giessen Hessen, Germany, had been in failing health for a year. He came to the United States when he was 23 years old and for many years worked in the experimental department of Bausch & Lomb Optical Company.

THEODORE M. BRUECK

In 1910 he and several associates founded what later was known as the Ilex Optical Company and went into the manufacture of camera wheel shutters, an invention of Mr. Brueck. Prior to his development of the wheel shutter, shutters on cameras were closed by pressing a small hand bulb. Mr. Breuck's invention made the closing automatic, by the use of gears and levers. The patent provided work for thousands of people.

My dad's father, Fred Carl, was born in Giessen, Germany. He had a brother, my great Uncle Teddy. Both had careers in optics. But something was happening in Germany that changed their lives.

In the early thirties, when they were young men, Hitler was rising to power. They, like many others, began to see a grim picture developing. The factories that were turning out cars and trucks began producing tanks and airplanes. They didn't like what they saw. It was time to leave.

My grandfather left first for the United States. Shortly after, his brother followed suit. They both eventually wound up in Rochester, New York. They began their new careers at Bausch & Lomb, which was famous for research and development in optics. Do you wear glasses? Take them off and look at them. You might find somewhere on them the names Bausch & Lomb.

Grandpa Fred was known worldwide as a specialist in quartz mineralogy. He traveled to many countries, especially Brazil, seeking the highest quality quartz crystals. Quartz was used then and is now used in making high quality prisms for binoculars, telescopes, and other optical instruments.

Many years ago quartz crystals were sawed into thin wafers of different thickness and were used in the early crystal radios. And Grandpa Fred worked on them. It was known then and now that if you submit an electrical current to a quartz crystal, the quartz crystal will oscillate at a constant frequency. If you sawed the crystal into thin wafers of different thickness and you applied an electric current to each of the thin wafers they would vibrate at different frequencies. And thus the crystal radio was born. If you turned the tuning knob on the radio you would get different radio stations.

I am being a little simplistic, but because of the expertise of people like Grandpa Fred, we have radios, binoculars, telescopes and many other products where quartz affects our daily lives.

Do you have a wrist watch or pocket watch on you now? Take a look at it. Does it say quartz on the dial? If so, the quartz crystal in your watch gives you the precise time until your battery goes dead. Because of their precision time keeping, quartz watches are more expensive.

I have a collection at home of many different sizes and shapes of quartz crystals that were willed to me by Grandpa Fred. The largest crystal I have is fifteen and one half inches long.

I became interested in rock and mineral collecting and have hundreds of different sized quartz crystals that I found locally by splitting open limestone rocks with a special rock hammer and assorted chisels.

Uncle Teddy, while still interested in optics, turned his attention to photography. He left Bausch & Lomb and founded the Ilex Optical Company. Get on the Internet and use a search engine (I use Google) and type in Ilex Optical Company. You should get "A History of the Rochester, NY Lens Companies." Click on Ilex and you will find Theodore Brueck there. Several of his co-workers joined him, but he was the one who came up with an idea that revolutionized the camera industry even to today.

He was the developer of the shutter camera. Prior to his invention shutters on cameras were closed by pressing a small hand bulb. His invention made the closing of the shutter automatic by the use of gears and levers. It was patented and provided work for thousands of people in the Rochester area. All cameras today, including the digital camera, still have that point and click shutter where you use your index finger and press the button.

Not as famous, but intelligent nonetheless, was Mom's father, Grandpa Bill, who worked for the Shinola Shoe Company. His invention, while simple, made opening a can of shoe polish easier. He got tired of using a coin or knife to open the two halves of the can. So he invented the "twistum," that separated the can halves.

Now for the rest of my family: My father was the dominant force in my life — in some good ways, but mostly bad. He was an intelligent, athletic outdoorsman who loved hunting and fishing. He went to the Eastman School of Music in Rochester, where he learned to play the piano. He ultimately played the piano to complement the silent movies in Rochester area theaters. He was a boxer and wrestler. He and several of his friends worked at a gym as trainers, where they had wrestling bouts with then-famous wrestlers like Strangler Lewis. He was employed as an accountant in Rochester during my early years until we moved to a farm in 1945 when I was nine years old.

Mom, on the other hand, was very quiet and shy. I took after her. Her mother, my grandmother, owned a tie shop in Rochester and was quite successful. But she had some qualities about her that turned people off. She was stubborn, bossy, and wasn't afraid to speak out and be critical of others. You will hear more about her later on.

I had one sibling, my sister Marilynn, whom I referred to as "Sis." As you will learn later Sis was born with asthma, a disease where the trachea (windpipe) and the bronchi (main airway) narrow due to some stimuli. That stimuli in our home was cigarette smoke. Pop smoked three packs a day and Mom smoked one pack a day. Sis was near death many times; my parents were partly responsible for that due to their smoking habit. At times Mom had to give Sis adrenalin sulfate shots to stimulate her heart to keep her alive until the ambulance came to take her to the hospital.

If you are a smoker, I beg you to kick the habit. Many people have tried to quit and failed. But remember: if you do quit, you may live a lot longer and the life you save may be your own or other family members that have to inhale the toxic smoke.

Mom's grandfather, my great-grandfather, was a pretty prolific guy. He was very tall, slender, and stately. He married a twin and they had six children. She died at an early age; eventually, he married the other sister and they had six children. He died at 102 years old!

I have a first cousin, Cathleen, whose husband, Chuck, had a rather interesting career. He worked for Carrier Corporation, the famous manufacturers of air conditioners in Syracuse, NY. He was an expert in solving air conditioning problems, even on submarines. He also worked for General Dynamics working on sonar for detecting

7

submarines. Today he travels anywhere as a consultant for air conditioning problems. He teaches courses at Syracuse University and Rensselear Polytechnic Institute in Troy, New York.

The other family members I have are my two second cousins, Evelyn, age 93, and Marcella, age 90 (who still drives a car).

According to Marcela, Pop and Mom were a perfect couple. In the early years of their marriage they were inseparable. Pop was an avid hunter and fisherman and Mom went with him most of the time. But there is more to the story.

So that leaves me as the only family member left; everybody is deceased, except my three cousins. The bottom line is my life, like anyone else's, has its ups and downs. While I am considered by my doctor to be in good health as far as my vital organs are concerned, I have had multiple medical problems, a few that I have had to deal with since birth.

I was born in 1936 and, unbeknownst to my parents, had spina bifida. The last vertebrae in my spine is missing. I was also born with a twist in my upper spine between the base of my skull and my shoulder blades. We didn't find this out until I was eleven years old when x-rays were taken because I was always complaining about the severe pain in my neck and lower back.

I am not crippled or handicapped; I can walk, run, and jump like most people. There is just that nagging pain that one has to accept and live with.

Perhaps this is one reason why I eventually became successful in my life. I had the will and determination to go on and be the best I could be.

My medical record reads like a horror story:

In the 60's I found out that I had stomach ulcers and benign prostate enlargement.

In the 70's I developed stomach and colon problems, but there was no specific diagnosis. I developed migraine headaches but I was able to control them by biofeedback. Osteoarthritis was added to the list in that decade as well.

In the 80's I had allergy tests, sixty of them, and I found out I had multiple allergies. The worst ones were dust, pollen, molds, and cat saliva. But I won't give up my little pussy cat; she is all I have left. I also found out I have multiple food intolerances, which came as no surprise to me, because almost anything I eat gives me problems.

In the 90's X-rays showed I had bone spurs growing on my spine; fifty-percent of the cartilage in my spine, from my belt line down, has disintegrated due to Osteoarthritis. I developed an irregular heartbeat, which I discovered was due to Seldane D, an anti-allergy drug. I fractured the ribs on my left side from a fall off a ladder in my barn. I got my fourth major concussion from a farm related accident in 1999.

In the year 2000 I was diagnosed with severe Irritable Bowel Syndrome, Barrett's Esophagus Disease and (last but not least) possible Crohn's Disease.

Have you had enough of this? So have I. But while life has not exactly been a picnic for me, I am one hell of a fighter. I won't give up. And that is the theme song of this whole book. *Never say can't.* I am living proof that life goes on and you make the best of it. In later chapters I will take you on some fabulous trips around the world. I have been to thirty-five foreign countries. You can't let a few aches and pains get you down.

CHAPTER 2
THE EARLY YEARS

As I mentioned, I had only one sibling, my sister Marilynn, or "Sis," as I called her. She had the misfortune of being born with asthma, and her story is one of suffering for most of her life. At times her face would turn blue and she would gasp to get air in her lungs. I remember Mom giving her adrenalin sulfate shots to stimulate her heart to keep her alive while waiting for the ambulance to take her to the hospital to stabilize her. From there, she was transferred to a former TB sanitarium where she literally lived in an oxygen tent, sometimes for weeks.

When she was well enough to come home, she had a tank of oxygen with an oxygen mask next to her bed to help her breathe, especially at night. Her bedroom door was always closed and I was not allowed in. I never figured out why I could not see her.

In grammar school I had all A's and A-pluses, while she had C's and D's. Why? She was smart, but she was out of school half of the time because of her asthma attacks. But guess what? She was a fighter, and never said "I can't." Sis kept at her studies and finally graduated from college.

Mom had her problems too. She was born with a birth defect, a spinal curvature in her upper back. It was quite obvious, and in public she always wore a shawl over her shoulders to hide her "hump back." I remember she frequently asked me, "Freddie, do I embarrass you?" I always answered, "Of course not, Mom." But I have to admit it did bother me that she was always in pain.

I was in pain as well with the Spina Bifida and the rotated spine. Often when we were walking to church my father would come up behind me and he would slap me on the upper back and say "stand up straight." I'd say, "I can't!" He would hit me again and repeat, "Stand up straight!" (Remember those words: "I can't." I'll be repeating them fairly often.)

Early on, Pop was a great dad. Before Sis and I were born, Pop and Mom bought a piece of land from a farmer and built their first house. We lived there for nine years, and as I grew older I noticed, at times, that Pop was acting rather strangely. Sometimes he would have a fight with Mom. At other times he would be a little unsteady when walking. I'd get scared and Sis would say, "It's OK, he just had a little too much wine." We did have a wine cellar in the basement. I'd go in there and watch the bubbles come up through a glass tube in the barrels. Come to think of it, I enjoyed that because I felt a little lightheaded from the sweet smell of fermenting grapes.

As time went on, it seemed Pop would visit the wine cellar more often and come staggering up the stairs. That was the beginning of a very poor relationship between the two of us.

One time, when I was in the first grade, we went for a short walk and he said something to me that was probably the beginning of my insecurities.

Pop and Mom were avid hunters and loved to go fishing, especially in Canada and Pop told me during our walk that I was not "planned." In other words, I was conceived in Canada...by mistake! That's a hell of a thing to tell a kid.

Pop with the catch of the day

Most kids might get a spanking if they do something wrong. Not this kid: If I misbehaved, he would go outside and pull down a small branch from one of our apple trees in the backyard. A side branch about two feet long and maybe one-quarter inch in diameter would be selected. He would cut it off and bring it into the house. He made me sit down on the couch in the living room. Taking his jack knife, which he always carried in his pants pocket, he would peel the bark off the twig. Then he would snap it against the couch to make a loud noise. I was next. One hit on the thigh would leave a red welt and I'd scream bloody murder.

There was another event that resulted in his favorite nickname for me. When I was about five years old I had a nightmare about a lioness chasing me. She was running at full speed and I was running as hard as I could — in slow motion. Suddenly the lioness stopped, squatted and urinated. At that point I woke up in a very wet bed. I, too, had urinated. From that point on, whenever we had a disagreement, my father's favorite name for me was "Piss Willy." Even when I was a teenager that was my name whenever he got mad at me.

left to right- cousin Cathy, Sis (holding rabbits), author

author, Sis, and Mom (holding a rabbit) resting on
one of the rabbit hutches

In order to increase the family income we raised hundreds of rabbits. They were kept in hutches in the back yard. We had about a dozen different breeds and they were sold for breeding and meat. The pelts were sold for fur gloves, hats and whatever else you can make from a dead rabbit.

Do you remember the movie *Bambi*? Remember Thumper, who would use one of his hind legs and rapidly strike the ground making a drumming noise? Well rabbits do that in real life too. There were times at night when you could hear them "thumping" whenever they sensed danger — like a stray dog in the neighborhood.

The rabbits were fed a specially formulated pellet food, which we bought in one-hundred-pound bags. Since this was during World

War II, the rabbit pellets came in cloth bags that had all kinds of fancy designs on them, like flowers and different prints. Mom used to make dresses, aprons and skirts from those fancy feed bags. These were tough times and people actually saved money by wearing a feed bag. We also took the fat from cooking meat, put it in tin cans and took them to the grocery store for the war effort.

One time, when he was drunk, Pop asked me if I would like to help him carry one of the hundred-pound bags of rabbit feed down some steep steps that led into the cellar. He was on the top step and I was two steps below him, walking backwards. Now I was only six years old, and when he suddenly lost his balance and pitched forward, I literally flew backwards down the stairs, landing on the concrete basement floor. My back struck the floor first, then my head, followed by that fancy 100 pound feed bag, which landed on top of me. I got an instant splitting headache and didn't know where I was or what happened. Mom heard the noise, ran down the stairs, screamed at Pop and literally picked me up in her arms (with her bad back and all) and carried me upstairs to the living room couch. That was the first of five concussions I got over the years (and they are accumulative). I won't repeat the cuss words Mom used when confronting Pop.

Now, a word about another family member I had to deal with: Granny. This was Mom's mom.

She was the second most influential person in my early life and, like my father, primarily in a negative way. All her attention was

16

focused on Sis. To her I was the healthy, shy brother. As explained in the next chapter, we moved and bought a farm when I was nine years old. On a Christmas afternoon, a truck pulling a trailer drove into the driveway with my grandmother following behind in her car. She came to the house and tapped on the window and told us to watch the trailer. I always felt "Granny" was a horse's ass, and guess what appeared? A horse's ass backing out of the trailer, and then the "whole horse" — a beautiful black mare with a white patch on her forehead. We named her Star. Here's the kicker: Granny came into the house, wished us all a Merry Christmas and then turned to me and said, "This is Sis's horse, not yours. It's for her to ride, not you." This was typical of her attitude towards me. Let's just say, I didn't cry at her funeral.

I did cry fairly often, though. I was very insecure and scared of just about everything, especially thunderstorms. Pop always used to tell me, "You're scared of your own shadow." One event that really used to scare me was the mock air raids over the city of Rochester, about 20 miles away.

Since I was born in 1936 and Sis in 1933, we were old enough to remember World War II. Aerial bombs were dropped with light explosives that gave the appearance of a Fourth of July celebration. But this was no celebration: It was serious stuff and it scared the hell out of me. I remember hiding behind the couch crying because I was so afraid. During these "air raids" everyone had to cover all the windows in the house with dark curtains, so that if we ever had a real

17

air raid, with real bombs, the enemy would not be able to see all the lights below to know that they were over a populated area where they could do great damage.

During this same time, my father became a volunteer air raid warden. He carried a Colt 45 pistol along with a flashlight on his rounds. His job was to go around the neighborhood and make sure all the houses were dark.

The farmer Pop bought the land from was nearby. The farmer had a black cat named Corky. As Pop was making his rounds one night, using his flashlight, he saw Corky. He bent down to pet her when he suddenly realized this wasn't Corky. It was a skunk! That was a stinking experience we never forgot!

two of the author's cows, age 13

Rusty, our riding horse

aftermath of a typical western New York State blizzard

Sis with one of her registered Guernsey calves

CHAPTER 3
THE FARM

When I was nine-years old, Pop decided we should move. He bought a farm about 30 miles from our first home. All our new neighbors were farmers.

Mom was not too thrilled about moving from a nice home to, as she put it, a "dump." It was a 100-year-old, two-story, four-bedroom house, and it was not in the best shape. The kitchen floor was wood planks and slightly tilted. One of the four bedrooms upstairs was made into a bathroom. The cellar had a dirt floor, a coal furnace and a cistern, which is a rectangular water storage facility built out of concrete blocks and plastered on the inside. Gutters along the roof collected rainwater and, by downspouts, the water emptied into the cistern. That water was used for taking a bath! One time a rat fell into the cistern and until we drained and scrubbed it clean, we took baths in that stinking water. No wonder mom wasn't thrilled about living in that house.

One of my best high school friends — of the few friends I did have — had a similar problem. A rat fell into the cistern in their cellar but there was a tragedy: His dad waded into the partially drained water to start cleaning the cistern. He had an extension cord with a light on it that he hung from the ceiling. The light fell into the water and he was electrocuted!

We had other water problems beside the cistern. We had two wells. One was for the house, and therefore right near the house. However, the well for the barn was about thirty feet from the barnyard and the manure pile. So you can guess what happens in the spring with the melting snow in the barnyard. The runoff, via underground veins, seeped into the well — and we drank that water! We had to boil it, then refrigerate it. Fortunately, since we had dairy cows we drank lots of milk. The house well was even worse. We had sulfur water. It was black and it stunk. Every so often when you turned the faucet on, black crud came spilling out. There was also sulfur gas in the water, so once in a while the water would "explode" out of the faucet and you would get an unexpected bath. You never left any silverware anywhere near the sink; if you did, you had to get out the silver polish to get the sulfur tarnish off.

By the way, we had a tin roof on the house and every time it rained hard you couldn't sleep due to the noise.

The farm had 100 tillable acres. That means that all the acreage, other than the farmstead, was good farm land and we could grow just about any kind of forage, grain or vegetable crop. We had fields to pasture the animals, as well as plenty of land upon which we could grow corn, wheat, hay, and kidney beans.

We had three large barns, the largest around. One barn was for the livestock. We had Holstein cattle, several pigs, always a riding horse and dozens of cats in that barn. The second story of the barn was for hay storage. I had to climb a vertical ladder attached to a wall to get to the hay mow to toss down bales for the cows, heifers, calves, and horse. (The pigs ate grain.) The cats kept happy with the milk and all those mice that every farm seems to have. The only problem was that, when you carried pails of milk to pour into the milk cans, the cats would run ahead of you. I can't count the number of times they tripped me up. Ever see a cat fly? They do when you give them a gentle lift off with your foot.

The second barn was also two stories. Downstairs we kept the family car, tractor, and all the machinery needed to do the field work. Upstairs we had a chicken coop with 300 Rhode Island Red hens that provided us with 300 eggs a day. There was a second part of the chicken coop where we raised baby chicks as replacements for the laying hens. We bought the chicks during the winter and they were kept in an area that had a brooder. The brooder had a heat lamp inside and it was suspended from the ceiling. It could be raised and lowered to regulate the temperature. The chicks had free run of this part of the barn, and could go under the brooder to stay warm.

Since you can't live on an all-egg diet, we sold the eggs to people in town. That meant that every day the eggs had to be graded by weight with, what else, but an egg scale. Then they had to be candled. This was done with a device with a built-in light that allowed you to see through the egg shell to detect anything abnormal, like blood spots. Then they were placed in cartons for sale. This was Mom's job and that was her spending money.

The third barn had a grain bin for storing wheat. Hay, plus straw from the wheat, was also stored in the barn. Since there was a lot of extra storage area, Pop let our farmer neighbors store their grain combines in the barn as well.

Back in those days farmers shared equipment. We did not have a spreader to spread manure from the livestock on to the fields so we borrowed one of our neighbor's spreaders. In turn, he stored his combine in our barn. Likewise, we did not have a front-end loader on our tractor to dig into the manure pile and dump it into the spreader, which would save a lot of back-breaking work with a pitch fork. So we borrowed another neighbor's tractor with a loader in exchange for his storing his combine in our barn. Today most farmers own all their equipment at a very high cost. A large combine can now cost in the hundreds of thousands of dollars.

Because we were relatively isolated and had no close neighbors, Pop began to drink more often. At times he got so drunk, he would literally pass out. I got less attention and our relationship was eroding. I also resented that most of his attention was on Sis because of her asthma.

But Sis and I always got along very well. We did a lot of things together. But living on a farm meant there was a lot of chores to do. I did most of the work because Sis was sick much of the time and Pop was blitzed. We had very little money because he spent most of it on booze. And because I didn't have any money to put away for college, except for the money I got for the milk from my cows, I began working for neighboring farmers at the age of 10.

Most of that work was out in the fields. For example, I would work weekends during the potato harvest season, picking up potatoes in a field for 10 cents a crate. It took about 20 minutes to fill a crate, which holds about 50 pounds of potatoes. Bending over all day was too painful because of my Spina Bifida. So I crawled on the ground to earn money. There is no such thing as can't. You can do it if you have to. And I had to work for my neighbors if I was to go to college. I also worked for a neighbor farmer who grew cabbage. I worked in those fields all day long bending over cutting heads of cabbage. Once cut, each cabbage head had to be thrown up to a guy in a truck. This was an all-day job, and there was no crawling on the ground for this kind work. It was literally a gigantic pain in the back. It was also a pain in the ass because I hated that job.

Despite the fact that I worked for neighbors, we did grow crops on our farm. They included hay, corn, wheat, and kidney beans. So I had to work in our fields but without pay. There is a saying: "It's a long row to hoe." I am not sure of its origin, but if you spent all day in the hot sun hoeing weeds out of the corn and bean rows in 20 acre fields, you'd understand that they really *were* long rows to hoe. We did have cultivators on our tractor that took the weeds out between the rows but not in the row where the crop was growing. And that's where you hoe those long rows. In those days we didn't learn about the danger of being out in the sun without sunscreen or protective clothing. I may be sorry sometime in the future because I worked outside in the sun all day without a shirt or hat on.

At the age of 11, I earned enough money to buy a Holstein heifer calf. When she came of age, I had her bred and she had a heifer calf. With time I had several milking cows. I was allowed to keep the milk money from these animals for college.

The only problem was I had to milk them before and after school. And I had to milk them by hand. I also had all the other chores to do. This included feeding the cows, heifers, calves, pigs, chickens, and horse. As a result, I never had any time in grammar or high school for extracurricular activities, and thus had few friends.

One of the non-extracurricular activities I had to do every day was "walk the plank." You remember those yarns about pirates making captives "walk the plank"? I actually did. Every day I had to shovel manure out of the gutters and into a wheel barrow, wheel it outside into the barnyard, and dump it in a pile. (Today farmers have mechanical gutter cleaners that take most of the hand work out of it.) As you keep dumping the manure every day the pile obviously keeps getting bigger. Eventually you have to set out a heavy 2x12 inch plank from the barn door to the top of the manure pile. Then you walk the plank to dump the manure on to the top of that ever-increasing pile.

CHAPTER 4

TERRORISM IN THE SCHOOL

When we moved to the farm, Sis and I obviously had to adjust to a new grammar school and new kids. Now we had to go to a Catholic grammar school, grades 4 to 8.

This was a completely different atmosphere than the public grammar school we went to before we moved to the farm. Kids will be kids and, at times, get into trouble. The teachers were nuns and they were always "patrolling the lane ways" between the rows of seats. If someone misbehaved, the kid was taken into the hall and slapped in the face, sometimes punched.

One of the tactics of a nun who taught 4th grade was to take a kid to the door that leads to the hallway, make him put his fingers between the door and the door jamb, and close the door on his fingers. Ever see four black-and-blue finger nails on one hand?

One time, when I was in the 7th grade, we were all outdoors and a couple of kids got into a fist fight. What usually happened on these "occasions" was all the kids formed a ring around the two combatants and cheered one or the other kid on. But this time it was in front of the rectory where the priest lived. Out came Father K running down the steps; he grabbed a kid and started punching him in the face, blood flying all over. The problem was he picked a kid who wasn't even in the fight.

I only got hit once. It was in the 5th grade, when the nun called me up to the blackboard. I was always very quiet and shy and was terrified of being called on. Because of that I always took the back seat in class. (Today I won't take the "back seat" to anyone.) So I reluctantly walked up to the blackboard and had to diagram a prepositional phrase. I went totally blank. The nun hit me across the shoulder blades where I had the rotated spine and I almost passed out from the pain.

But it wasn't all bad. The nuns taught discipline in school, and I think we need more of that today.

My best experience in grammar school was in the eighth grade. All the kids in the Catholic Diocese of Rochester had to write a composition on "the reasons why I want to go to summer camp."

I thought to myself, "I can't do that." I was horrible in writing book reports. There was no way I could do that. Well, I made an attempt because I had to; it was a class project and it was required. About a month later Sister E stood in the front of the class and announced the winner of the essay. There could only be one winner in the entire Catholic diocese. And I won! Wow! There really is no such word as can't. This was one of the turning points in my life. I suddenly realized my father was right: You can do it. It's all a matter of attitude.

When it was time for my parents to drive me to the camp I was sick to my stomach. This would be the first time I would be away from home. The camp was on one of the Finger Lakes in

Central New York State. After they left I never felt so lonely in my life. After several days I got used to my surroundings and actually started talking to some of the kids. You had to sign up for extracurricular activities, and for some reason I signed up for a "learn to swim" class. Perhaps it was because one time Sis nearly drowned in Lake Ontario.

On one particular day that I will never forget, I came back from one of my swimming lessons and hung my wet trunks on a railing on a screened-in porch where we slept at night. I laid down on my bed and fell asleep. When I awoke and got up a big kid, who was a bully, came down the porch hallway and stopped by my bed. He took my bathing trunks off the railing and threw them on the floor. Then he just looked at me in defiance. For some reason I said, "Pick them up and put them back on the railing." Without saying a word he picked them up, walked over to me and, with a mighty swing of his arm, slapped me in the face with the trunks. It almost knocked me down. Then I did something I never did before: I punched him in the face. I hit him in the left eye and immediately it started to swell. I thought, now I'm the one who is going to get hurt. But it never happened. He turned around and ran down the hall.

The next morning he came back to the hall where I slept, and as he approached me, I could see his eye was completely closed and was black and blue. I expected the worst but he extended his right arm and shook my hand and said, "I'm sorry." I was dumbfounded. We soon became friends. That episode was another turning point in my life. I finally stood up for my own rights. I began to develop some self-confidence; unfortunately, I had to hit someone to gain that confidence.

CHAPTER 5
BOYHOOD FRIENDS

Because of my insecurity, self-consciousness, and a feeling of being left out, thanks to Pop and Granny, I had few friends in school.

But I do have a lifelong friend, John. Even though we are miles apart today, we still communicate and reminisce about the good old days.

John's and our farm were back to back so it was easy to get together. But it seems every time we saw each other we got into some kind of mischief.

One day John drove over with his parent's tractor. I was out in a field picking up stones with our tractor, which was the same make and model as theirs.

John said, "Let's have a drag race." I said, "I can't. I have to finish picking stones." "Come on!" he said. So we had a drag race. But the place we chose was a big mistake.

Several years before this event, I had planted 1,000 Christmas tree seedlings by hand as a 4-H project. Now they were about two feet tall. So was the grass and weeds in this "mini" forest. I totally forgot about those trees.

With our tractors side by side, throttles wide open, we raced down our "tree lined drag strip". John won the race but I lost ten percent of my trees! The survivors were later cut and sold for Christmas trees when I was home from college for the Christmas break. That was one time I should have stuck to my favorite phrase: "I can't": I don't have the time to drag race.

There was one time when we decided to play "circus tight rope walker." The horizontal beams in our barns were at least one foot square. So there was a 12 inch "wire" we could walk along. I went about 50 feet, lost my balance, fell 15 feet, and landed on my left side. I didn't break any bones but I got my second major concussion.

John was a "trickster." One time we were playing in our haymow and decided to have a rope climbing contest. There were several large manila ropes hanging from the peak of the barn ceiling. At the count of three, I climbed up the rope and reached the top first. John didn't even climb the other rope. He was laying on his side on the barn floor groaning. I slid down the rope and asked him if he was OK. He turned his head to me and it was covered with blood. I was horrified. Then he suddenly started to laugh. This was another one of his tricks. He had a small packet of ketchup and had smeared it on his face! Fond memories of bygone days.

Now for the bad news. As a farm boy, like me, John had to do morning and evening chores milking the cows. One hot summer afternoon when he was milking the cows, a thunderstorm was brewing. It was approaching fast and John went to close the barn windows. There was a steel cable on the outside of the barn by the window, and as he reached up to close the window, lightning struck the transformer by the road. The charge traveled to the barn wires and then to the steel cable. The lightning strike literally threw him backwards. He landed in the manure gutter behind the cows, unconscious and stiff as a board, with his arms outstretched. His dad raced to the barn and they took him to the hospital.

After many tests, doctors found that much of the nerves throughout his body were burned. There were many years of pain and therapy. But John, like me, was a fighter. He eventually became successful in the insurance business.

John on Rusty; left to right: Shep, the author, sis and Togi

There is one other thing. John learned early on that there is no such word as "I can't." He struggled for many years like me, but under different circumstances. But he never gave up. Neither did I.

One of the many problems of having an alcoholic father was his control over me. I was not allowed to have or do many of the things that other kids did, like having a driver's license and a car.

I had several other friends, Tommy and Louie. They were sixteen, the same age as I was at that time. They both had cars. How could sixteen-year-olds afford a car? Like me, they worked as farm boys at home and got paid for helping do chores and other farm related jobs.

However, being friends, Tommy and Louie would call me up at different times and I would go cruising in their customized cars.

What is a customized car? Back in those days all cars had hood and trunk ornaments. They "had" to be removed. The holes were filled in and painted over.

Next, you had to put fender skirts on the rear fender panels. These panels hid the rear wheels. Does that make any sense? No, but it was cool! Then you put in lowering blocks to lower the back end of the car. That made it look like the car was going uphill when it was on a flat road. That doesn't make any sense either. But it looked good to us. Finally you modified the exhaust system by adding a second head pipe and tail pipe with a "Hollywood" muffler in between. The cool phrase was "dual mufflers". The louder, the better. I loved to ride in their loud customized racing machines.

Suddenly these Saturday night cruises ended. They discovered girls! Yes, now Tommy and Louie could take their girlfriends, find a secluded place, and "park." You know the rest of the story. So now, on Saturday nights, which was date night, poor Freddie would go up to his room and play solitaire. It sure would have been more fun to play with a girlfriend. But back then I was too shy and introverted to go out anyway. By the way, I still play solitaire on my computer. Playing regular card games helps keep my brain stimulated so hopefully I won't get Alzheimer's disease like my grandfather Fred Carl, who died from it. Working on a puzzle is also believed to help, but I don't play with puzzles. My life has been one big puzzle and that's enough to deal with.

CHAPTER 6

THE HIGH SCHOOL YEARS

I had three problems in high school: English, history, and math.

English was particularly bad, especially when we had to do book reports. I "just didn't get it." And I never asked for help. So now I'm writing a book? Figure that one out. I can't!

I thought history was boring and math was something I could get along without. Wrong! I found out later in my professional career that I had to use math quite often and regretted not doing my homework. As far as history is concerned, to me it was past history and that's the end of it.

My favorite, and most practical course, was in Vocational Agriculture. I learned more there than in any other course and it was a great help in my professional career. I took 3 years of VoAg and each year I got 100 on my final exam. You can do it if you try hard.

As I indicated before, I missed out on a lot of extracurricular after school activities.

But in my junior year I did try out for the baseball team as a pitcher. I had excellent control, but not enough speed on the ball.

Back in grammar school we had a kid, Bobby, who could throw a softball underhand, faster then the fastest kid throwing a hard ball overhand. In high school, Bobby was the star hard ball pitcher and drew national attention. There were overflow crowds at every game. No one could hit the ball with his blazing speed. He pitched 22 straight winning games. 18 were no hitters! All the major baseball teams had scouts watching him at each game. Eventually he was signed by the Saint Louis Cardinals.

I understand there is a plaque about Bobby's feats in the Baseball Hall of Fame in Cooperstown, New York. It is a forty minute drive from my home. I have been to Cooperstown many times but I have never visited the Hall of Fame.

I could have done much better in high school than I did. Several teachers told my mother, "Freddie has the ability, he just doesn't apply himself." Part of it was I was bored. I cannot remember, in all my years in both grammar and high school, any teacher that really inspired me. Most were dull and boring. The best teacher is a motivator. He or she can motivate the kids to want to learn and excel. Unfortunately they are few and far between. If I had my way, and was on a school board, I would fight for paying the motivational teachers top salary, not those with seniority.

In school I never asked for help when I had a question or problem with an assignment. To make matters worse, I usually sat in the back seat in class because I was so shy. The worst part of my problem was I could not read the writing on the black board. (Why are they called black boards? Today many schools have green boards. Should they call them green black boards? Back to the drawing boards.) Even if I squinted, I had trouble seeing the board. Mom took me to an eye doctor in my freshman year in high school and I was given corrective glasses to wear. Wow, what a difference! But guess what? I never wore them. I was too self-conscious. If I had worn them I would have been a straight A student.

Parents, if you have a child in school and, if like me, they won't wear their glasses when they need to, please do everything in your power to convince them to wear them. It can make an important difference in their life.

I think I was one of the few kids in high school that never dated. But I did have one date the very last day. Barbara was a very nice girl, but like me, she was very quiet and shy. She asked me if I would take her to the senior prom. A girl asking a boy? Shouldn't it be the other way around? Not with this kid! I came up with every excuse I could think of as to why I could not go to the prom. I told my mother about it and she lit into me like I never saw her do before. "You take her to the prom! You need to get out and meet girls. If you don't some day you are going to be very sorry. You might meet the wrong one and you will regret it." In retrospect — right on, Mom! (You'll read all about that later on.)

I can't recall much of what happened that night. I did take her to the prom. I do remember I had an upset stomach, my hands were freezing and I had a headache. I also remember that we just stood in one spot and I moved my feet a little but we weren't going anywhere. If any other part of my body was moving it was probably from shaking because of my frazzled nerves! In a later chapter you will learn more about another kind of dancing; there may have been a few times when I danced around someone's question in my professional career when I didn't know the proper answer!

CHAPTER 7

SUMMER JOBS

After graduating from high school in 1954, I desperately needed a summer job to earn money for college in the fall. I applied to go to Cornell University and I was accepted. There were few jobs at that time but I found one working at my hometown lumber yard. It was probably one of the worst decisions I ever made. I was now 18 and I finally got a driver's license and bought a used car.

1954 was one of the hottest summers on record. My first job was unloading railroad box cars full of, what else, lumber. Can you imagine what it is like to break the seal on the locked doors of the boxcar, open the door and feel the blast of hot air in your face? Even worse, entering the box car was like hell on earth. There was no air in there; it was sweltering. Within fifteen minutes after I started unloading 2x4's, 2x6's, 2x8's, and 2x10's, I was soaking wet. Even my belt and shoes were wet. About every two hours the owner/manager of the lumberyard would bring me water to quench my thirst and give me raisins for energy. The lumber I was handling was handed off to a guy who loaded them on a lumber truck that was backed up to the box car door. When loaded, we drove the truck to an area in the lumber yard where the lumber was off loaded, and stacked in piles. All summer long the outdoor temperature was in the high eighties to the low to mid nineties. Toward the end of the summer I "graduated" to driving that lumber truck for delivering lumber to house building sites.

Of course I had to load the truck and drive it to the site. Loading a truck has to be done properly. The first thing I learned was you never lay a window or door with glass panels flat. It has to be set upright. The first delivery I made, I placed a door with glass panels flat on the truck. Hitting the first bump in the road, I heard the crash, tinkle-tinkle of breaking glass. Boy was I glad when that job ended.

Between my sophomore and junior year I had a summer job working on a farm about ten miles from our farm. Since I had gone to college and I was no longer home, except for the summers, all the livestock was sold. There was no one to do the chores anymore. I also had to sell my cows. I had a bull calf that I had registered with the Holstein Breed Association and a dairy farmer from New Jersey bought him for $200. That was a lot of money in those days.

The best and most interesting summer job was between my junior and senior year at Cornell. I was lucky to get a job at the Rochester Gas and Electric (RG&E) an electric power generating station by Lake Ontario. In order to get the job I had to be investigated by the Federal Bureau of Investigation. The FBI! Why? If anyone wanted to do a dastardly deed, one of the best places to do the most damage is to attack a power generating plant. This was a coal burning plant. Coal was delivered to the plant from Pennsylvania or Ohio by railroad. There were scores of loaded railroad coal cars in the rail yard. The railroad cars were bottom unloaded and moved by conveyor inside the plant where it was "fed" to four huge furnaces. The burning coal heated the water that was pumped into the station via large pipes from Lake Ontario. The heated water was converted into steam. The steam was piped to four huge turbines. The steam was forced into fan blades on the turbines which turned the turbine shafts. The revolving turbine shafts were connected to the four generators. The generators produced the electricity. The electricity was directed to an outdoor grid system that distributed it via transmission lines to Rochester and the greater Rochester area. Sounds simple but you would not believe the miles of piping and the hundreds of pumps and compressors that were an integral part of turning those turbines and generators.

My first job in this four-story plant was to make the rounds every hour for eight hours a day to check each compressor and pump and make sure they were running okay and not overheating. If there was a problem I called the foreman and he and his crew would fix it.

I remember the first day after the foreman showed me around, discussing what I was supposed to do, he said, "Oh by the way, watch out for Louie." What the hell did that mean? A few days later I found out. Instead of climbing flights of stairs to get to the fourth floor, I took the elevator. When the door opened there was a man already in there. I said, "Hi!" and turned around to push the fourth floor button. Suddenly he came up behind me and put one arm around my chest and the other right on my crotch! Ah ha, that had to be Louie! I stomped on his right foot, wheeled around, and grabbed

43

him by the throat with my left hand. With my right fist poised ready to hit him I said, "If you ever try that again you're dead." He turned white, ran to the door, pushed a button and ran out. I never saw him again.

From that time on I did my dutiful job of checking the pumps and compressors. Boring, but the pay was good. What wasn't good were the eight hour shifts. One week I worked from 7:30 am to 3:30 pm, the next week 3:30 pm to 11:30pm, and the third week from 11:30 pm to 7:30 am. After the first few weeks I had a terrible time getting to sleep. When I got up I was so groggy I could hardly function. This went on for the full time I was on the job. I never said, "I can't." I just toughed it out, being thankful that I had a job.

Besides making the rounds, the other major job was to "shoot the furnaces." No not bang bang! It was with water. With any coal furnace you to have to dispose of the clinkers, or remains, of the burnt coal. At home with our coal furnace, you had a steel handle that you used to move the grates back and forth for the clinkers to drop through the grates to the bottom of the furnace. You simply opened a door at the bottom and with a shovel put the clinkers in a pail to take away for disposal.

With those four gigantic furnaces it was impossible to do that, so you used jets of water to clean them out. It took two men to use a huge wrench to open several water valves. This allowed heavy streams of water into the furnace to float the clinkers out a door in the bottom of the furnace. You really had to know what you were doing:

Too much water at the wrong place or at the wrong time meant the clinkers could build up by the clinker exit door. They could form a dam and then you were real in trouble.

Toward the end of my job, before returning to Cornell, I was promoted to work in the turbine room. Now that was interesting. My job was to read and record literally hundreds of dials and gauges that measured temperature, rpm's (or speed of the revolving shafts on the four generators and four turbines), voltage meters, and the list goes on. I even had to check and record the eccentricity of the revolving shafts. Ah ha! I'll bet I got you on that one. Eccentricity measures any wobbling of the shafts on the generators or turbines. It's like spinning a top when you were a kid. Initially it spins around but, as the momentum decreases, the top slows down and begins to wobble on its axis and then falls over. Any wobbling of the shafts will cause wear and that will cause vibration, which spells trouble. The generator or turbine then has to be shut down and repaired. And that's a major project.

I hope from all of this you have a greater appreciation of what goes on behind the scenes when you flip on that light switch. All in all it was an interesting job, despite that horrible time schedule.

CHAPTER 8

LITTLE MAN ON THE BIG CAMPUS

When I was in grammar school and high school, my father kept saying he wanted me to go to college at Cornell. I always told him I didn't have any money and neither did he. My biggest concern was how was I ever going to get into Cornell. I could work my way through college, which I did, but I could never get in there. Besides it is too big a University. I'm too shy to make any new friends. I came up with all kinds of excuses. But despite my lack of self confidence and all the other negatives I was accepted.

In September 1954 I drove to Ithaca with a lump in my throat much of the way. This would be the first time I would be away from home for a long while.

I will be mentioning Cornell many times as you read on so I want to introduce you to this world famous university.

Cornell is one of eight universities in the Ivy League. The other seven are Harvard, Yale, Princeton, The University of Pennsylvania, Brown, Columbia, and Dartmouth.

They are called the Ivy League Universities because it was agreed upon by the presidents of these eight institutions that intercollegiate football would be maintained to keep the values of the game, but they also wanted to keep in perspective the main purpose of academic life: teaching students.

There was always rivalry when it came to sports. I attended many of those competitive games. The one I remember most vividly was a non-Ivy League game between Cornell and Syracuse University.

To say that Cornell was the underdog is an understatement. When I was a freshman, the legendary Jim Brown played fullback for Syracuse. I will never forget watching him carry the ball, dragging three Cornell players down the field. I think the score was something like 50 to 0. And if I remember correctly, he did most of the scoring.

A little bit more about Cornell: It is made up of six colleges and two schools. The colleges are Agriculture and Life Sciences, Architecture, Arts and Planning, Arts and Science, Engineering, and Human Ecology. The two schools are Hotel Administration and Industrial and Labor Relations.

Within these two colleges and schools, there are around 85 different disciplines from agriculture to urban and regional studies.

The following is a listing, from Cornell's web site, of the different majors one can presently take in the College of Agriculture and Life Sciences: Animal Sciences, Applied Economics and Management, Atmospheric Science, Biological and Environmental Engineering, Biological Sciences, Biology and Society, Biometry and Statistics, Communication, Crop and Soil Sciences, Education, Entomology, Food Science, International Agriculture and Rural Development, Landscape Architecture, Natural Resources, Nutrition Food and agriculture, Plant Sciences, Rural Sociology, and Science of Earth Systems.

While I took some individual courses from those I listed, I concentrated on four disciplines: Animal Science, Crop and Soil Sciences, Farm Business Management, and Agricultural Engineering. Ironically, these four disciplines were the areas of expertise that I was responsible for in my thirty-three year career, initially as a county-employed Cornell Cooperative Extension Agent and later as a Cornell-employed Regional Extension Specialist.

Cornell has had its share of world renowned professors. The two famous ones I remember, but never met, were Carl Sagan and Hans Bethe.

Carl Sagan was the David C. Duncan Professor in Physical Sciences at Cornell. He was a visionary astronomer with special interests in studying the universe. You may remember his remarkable television documentary series, "Cosmos."

I saw Hans Bethe many times on campus. He was a nuclear physicist who, among many accolades, won the Nobel Peace Prize for calculating the precise fusion reactions that power the stars in our universe. He worked on the Manhattan Project with Oppenheimer, Teller and Fermi that ultimately resulted in the development of the atomic bomb.

Life on campus can have its problems. My first week at Cornell, I made a left turn into a parking lot. As I was making that turn, a car was coming out of the parking lot. He smashed his car into the left side of my car with a mighty crash. Some kid in a hurry? Guess again. It was a professor in a big hurry. The car was damaged enough that I had to get another used car. I found out about a little old lady, if you can believe this, who owned a black 1950 Pontiac convertible with a white canvas top. The price was right so I bought it, and now I was the big man on the big campus.

I lived in the dorms during my freshman year. From my sophomore through my senior year I lived in the basement of a rather wealthy family. I had the same roommate, Art, for all four years. Art and I did not have to pay any money for our room in the basement, which I often referred to as the "dungeon." We just had to keep the house and property neat and squeaky clean.

Art was a smart kid. He hardly ever studied. Because of his influence on me I goofed off a lot as well. His father was a Cornell graduate. According to Art, his dad had the second highest average ever in the College of Agriculture.

You may recall that I had only one date in high school and that was more of a traumatic experience than a date should ever be. What about my dating at Cornell? In my freshman year in the dorms, Frank, who befriended me, was in a room down the hall. One time he asked me if I would double date with him. You haven't heard this for awhile: "I can't. I have home work to do." Frank had a girlfriend and he said he had a date for me. Help! I came up with more excuses but finally gave in. This would be the second date in my whole young life. We went to a movie in downtown Ithaca. On the way back to the campus, for some reason, I asked my date for her phone number. A month later, after much thought, I called her and asked if she would like to go to the movies on Saturday night. Her was response was, "Thank you but actually I am married"! My shocked response was "sorry!" and I hung up.

As a matter of interest: the city of Ithaca is right at the end of Cayuga Lake, one of the five Finger Lakes in central New York State. The Cornell campus looks down on the lake. These five lakes, when you fly over them or look at a map, are spread out like the five fingers on your hand. That's why they are called the finger lakes. By the way, there is a song they used to play at football games but the kids turned the lyrics around a little: "Far above Cayuga's waters, there's an awful smell. Some say it's Cayuga's waters, some say it's Cornell."

My next dating experience was even worse than the previous one. Three guys from down the hall asked me if I would like to quadruple date. I never heard of quadruple dating, I just made it up. One of the guys said, "We'll call Cortland State Teachers College and have the house mother in the dorm round us up four chicks." I was about to say, "I can't I have a prelim Monday," but I thought, this has got to be better than that married woman. So we went to Cortland.

When we arrived and found the dorm, one of the guys talked to the house mother and asked her to make a phone call to see if the girls were ready. Five minutes later three beautiful chicks and one ugly duckling came down the stairs. The three guys each grabbed a chick and I wound up with the ugly duckling. I was about ready to quack up! We went to an ice cream parlor and filled up on shakes and hamburgers, talked (except for me), and drove the girls back to the dorm. I didn't date again until my junior year.

One fateful time in my junior year, Art said, "Fred, I'm going to the 4-H Club meeting on campus tonight. Come with me." Here we go again. He finally talked me into it, which I regretted years later. After the formal meeting there were refreshments. A girl came over to me and asked me if I would like some cookies. I said sure. I guess that's the way the cookie crumbles. We talked for several hours. That never happened to me. She was nice and easy to talk to. The next Friday I asked her if she would like to go to the movies on Saturday night. Why do guys always want to go to the movies? Probably, for me, so I would not have to keep thinking up things to say or talk about.

We hit it off pretty well and went steady from my junior year through my senior year. We talked about getting married after I graduated. I wasn't ready for that responsibility but she was. I gave in and we got married in September, 1958. Her parents were very upset because she was a junior and that meant that she would not get her BS degree. Several years after we were married, she went back to Cornell on weekdays, came home on weekends, and got her BS.

Pop with Shep, with Togi; watching

CHAPTER 9

DOGS, PLANES, GUNS AND ALCOHOL

There were a number of family pets in my life. We had dogs from the time I was a toddler through high school. Cats entered into my life when I built my house in 1967 when a stray cat appeared one day and I took him in. But this chapter is about dogs.

When I was a small child, we had several beautiful Irish Setters. On rare occasions, Pop would ask me if I would like to go pheasant hunting with Timmy and Tammy. They would walk ahead of us. Suddenly they would stop and point with one front foot up and tail straight out, standing perfectly still. This was our signal that there were birds ahead. Pop would give them a command and they would flush them out. As soon as the pheasants were airborne, they were dead ducks…oops, I mean dead pheasants.

Later we had a Labrador Retriever. This dog was for duck hunting. Pop hand carved and painted all his duck decoys. He really was good at it. From a distance they were a spitting image of a real duck. I used to stand there at his workbench and watch him work for hours. On occasion, I would go duck hunting with him, sitting freezing in a duck blind. He had a duck call, you know, quack, quack. Some ducks would fly by and begin circling, then, bang, bang, bang and three dead ducks would hit the water. Immediately the lab swam out and retrieved the ducks.

I was impressed by the intelligence of these dogs but I never became a hunter for the sport of it. But later when I started raising sheep and coyotes killed some of my adult sheep and lambs, I became a revengeful hunter.

One solution to this problem is to get a guard dog. There are special breeds of dogs that do not become pets. At all times they stay with the sheep flock guarding them from predators.

The worst enemy for any shepherd and his or her sheep is the domestic dog. Coyotes will kill to get a meal and only kill one or two at a time. However, your pet dog can cause devastating damage. One domestic dog, a family pet, can kill 30 sheep or more, at one time. They start by running and chasing the sheep. When they catch the first one and draw blood, they become killing machines. Instinct takes over and they take down one sheep after another. So be aware.

If you have a dog or dogs and live in the country, and your neighbor has a sheep flock, that nice, friendly neighbor has every right to kill your dog if it runs his or her sheep.

When Pop bought our farm, Shep, a mixed breed, came with the farm. She soon bonded to me and never let me out of her sight. No matter where I was or what I was doing, she would be with me. I remember plowing fields in the spring, preparing the soil for planting. Shep would walk endlessly in the furrow behind the plow waiting for a mouse to show up.

Shep had one bad habit: she would hunt for woodchucks. Among the crops we grew were dry beans, otherwise known as kidney beans. We lost a lot of beans from those woodchucks. I'd shoot them, and Shep would pick them up and carry them off. Where? She would bury them in the manure pile in the barnyard and let them "cook". The more rotten the smell, the better they were — for Shep. She'd roll in the carcass after she dug it up, then dine out somewhere under a shade tree. You always knew where she was after she dug one up. You didn't have to look for her. Just follow the stench.

Enter Togi. While Shep was the family dog, one of Pop's friends asked if we would adopt his collie, Togi. Reluctantly, Pop agreed and now we had the rivalry between Shep and Togi. They soon settled their differences and became friends.

Togi bonded to Sis, just like Shep bonded to me. But Togi had a problem we didn't know about: she chased cars. Now why would a dog chase cars? They can't catch them. Suppose they did. What would they do with it? Bite the tires? The big car chase became her downfall.

I was in college when I got the letter from Mom. It was really sad.

One day, Togi was chasing a car. Pop was outside drunk as a skunk. Mom was in the house and heard a loud noise. She said it sounded like a gun going off. She went to the window and Pop, staggering, had shot Togi with his pistol. Mom screamed at him when she saw Togi yelping and crawling towards him. She said it was like the dog was begging for mercy. He shot again and missed. A third shot and he hit her again. Mom was helpless to do anything for fear he would, in his enraged and drunken stupor, aim the pistol at her. One more shot and Togi lay motionless. Mom never told Sis what really happened; she just said Togi was killed by a car.

There was another incident that made me very angry but had nothing to do with dogs. It was about planes and guns.

When I was a kid, I used to build model airplanes. Some were stick and paper models. Others I carved out of balsa wood with a knife, using templates to carve the wood to the proper shape. The stick and paper models were rather fragile but were easier to make, at least for me. After I finished each plane I would hang it from the ceiling of my bedroom at various angles with fishing line and small finishing nails.

When my grandfather Fred Carl died, he willed me his rock and mineral collection, two World War One army rifles and one Revolutionary War flintlock rifle with the ram rod and hammer you cocked back with your thumb. This rifle was worth a lot of money.

One time, between semesters, I left Cornell to go home and visit. Arriving late in the afternoon, after greeting Mom and Sis, (Pop was asleep in his chair, probably passed out as usual from drinking) I went up to my room to empty my suitcase. When I opened the door and looked around, everything was gone: the airplanes, the two army rifles and, yes, the Revolutionary War rifle too. I couldn't believe it. Mom entered the room crying, and said, "I'm so sorry, Freddie. He took them and sold them for booze money." She also told me for the first time that she would have left Pop, taking Sis and me with her but she wanted to keep the family together.

Now these are just several examples, among many, of how demented and selfish an alcoholic can become. So here is my appeal to you or someone you know who is an alcoholic:

Alcoholism can rarely be cured. It can only be managed. How? Alcoholics Anonymous. Pop never considered it, but we begged him to go. He never did. So I beg you to help a family member or friend you know that has this horrible problem. They are in denial and normally will not listen to your pleas. But they just might listen to a fellow alcoholic who might offer them some help and encouragement.

I am quoting from the Alcoholics Anonymous web site: "AA is a fellowship of men and women who share their experience, strength and hope with each other that they may solve their common problem and help others to recover from alcoholism. The only requirement for membership is to stop drinking. There are no dues or fees for AA membership; we are self-supporting through our own contributions. AA is not allied with any sect, denomination, politics, organization or institution. AA does not wish to engage in any controversy, neither endorses nor opposes any causes. Our primary purpose is to stay sober and help other alcoholics to achieve sobriety."

I have one other thought: all kids need a father, just like they need a mother. I had a father but I had no respect for him. But before he came under the domination of the bottle he was a good dad. As you have learned, he became a monster and I hated him. But at least I did have a father. There lots of kids who never had a dad. I feel badly for them.

author leaving "the box" for work

CHAPTER 10

LIVING IN THE BOX

Having graduated from Cornell and now married, I desperately needed a job. But we were in a recession and there were few jobs available. Most importantly, we needed a place to live that we could call "home." Renting an apartment was not an option. You can not build equity by renting. How about a mobile home? The advantage of mobile home living is obvious. Your home is mobile; you can move it to a mobile home court or trailer court. Or one could buy a plot of land, if it is zoned for mobile homes, and have some privacy on one's own property. Since I had no money I got a bank loan and purchased a new ten-foot by forty-five-foot mobile home and we moved to a trailer park in Johnstown, New York, in Fulton County.

Trailer parks are not exactly my favorite place to live. You can have very nice neighbors or the worst. The worst one was right across from us, which was about 20 feet away. One Sunday afternoon "he" was in the back seat of his car on top of some woman. They were not playing "tiddly winks." At the same time "she" was beating up one of the kids. You could hear the slapping and punches. The cops came and took care of the situation. Trailer court living had its ups and downs, no pun intended, but we coped with it.

Johnstown is not that far from the Adirondack Mountains. I was always interested in rock and mineral collecting and the Fulton County Rock and Mineral Club was nearby, so I joined. I went on quite a few rock hunting expeditions and collected many different kinds of rocks of various sizes and colors.

After three years we decided to move. We wanted more breathing room. The mobile homes were too close together for this farm kid, so we moved our home to Randall, New York, in Montgomery County, where there was more space. A big plus was the fact that we had free access to a swimming pool.

The rocks I had collected took up a lot of room. There was a gravel pit across the road. I figured it would not do any harm to dump some of the rocks in the gravel pit and scatter them around a bit.

Some time later a high school teacher took his science class on a field trip. One of the stops was the gravel pit. He wanted to teach the students about the different kinds of stones and rocks native to our area. He let the students go on their own for a while to look around and see how many different kinds of stones they could find. Soon he was inundated with kids going crazy over the treasures they found. He was unable to explain how all those different kinds and colors of rocks could possibly be there. I'll bet he thought he must have been "stoned," thinking about what happened that day at that gravel pit.

CHAPTER 11

MY FIRST PROFESSIONAL JOB

In 1958 we were in a recession and jobs were scarce. I wanted and needed a job where I would be able to utilize my farm background and Cornell education.

There was an opening in Montgomery County in upstate New York for an Assistant County Agricultural Agent position with Cornell Cooperative Extension. The office was about six miles from Johnstown where I lived, so that was a big incentive to consider applying for the job.

Not everyone understands what Cooperative Extension is or what it does. So here's a bit of history.

Remember "Honest Abe"? Well, at least you do from the history books. In 1862, President Lincoln set up the Morill Act, which essentially purchased and set aside a plot of land in every state in the United States to found a university dedicated to agriculture and mechanical arts. They were to be called Land Grant Colleges. For example, In New York State Cornell is the Land Grant College. In Oregon it is Oregon State University. In New Mexico it is New Mexico State University. In California it is the University of California at Davis. You get the picture.

There were three basic things that these universities must do.

First: Provide resident instruction, which means teaching students on campus.

Second: Do basic research. Find answers and solutions to unsolved problems.

Third: Extend the teaching and research beyond the university to all the people in each state.

Author's First Day At Work

New Assistant County Agriculture Agent Appointed

Frederick L. Brueck has been named assistant county agricultural agent replacing James H. Gould, Jr., who recently became county 4-H agent, according to G. Edson Bowers, St. Johnsville, chairman of the Agricultural Extension Service Executive Committee. The appointment was effective June 23.

Brueck received his bachelor of science degree in General Agriculture at Cornell last month. He is a native of Monroe County and was raised on a 100 acre general cash crop and dairy farm.

In 4-H club work, Brueck started out with one heifer and built up a herd of purebred Holsteins. He was active in the FFA, participating in field and forage crop projects and dairy judging teams.

While at Cornell, he majored in General Agriculture and included animal husbandry, agronomy, agricultural engineering, veterinary medicine, vegetable crops and horticulture in his curriculum. He was active in the campus 4-H club, vegetable crops club and Newman Club. In Dec. 1957, he placed first on the Cornell vegetable crops judging team and was sent to the National Intercollegiate Vegetable Judging contest in New Orleans, La.

Thus Cooperative Extension was born. The word Cooperative indicates that there is cooperation between the university and federal, state and county governments to fund the programs.

The word Extension indicates that the University research and teaching is extended beyond the University out to all the people in the state.

Cooperative Extension Agents, representing the University, are hired to help bring about change by providing new ideas and programs that will benefit and improve the lives of the people they serve. They carry these programs out in many ways: mass media, which includes newspaper releases, radio, and television programs; newsletters; seminars; one-on-one counseling on the farm, in the office, or over the telephone; field demonstration; research trials; and the list goes on.

Three weeks after the position was announced, I went for an interview. I got the job.

One big plus about my new job was that the office was only six miles from our home in Johnstown. The big minus was the building I worked in. It was a Greek Revival style stone structure with large windows that went up almost to the ceiling. Combining a building made out of stone, with lots of glass, means you froze in the winter time. Not only that, but the main tracks of the New York Central Railroad were about fifty feet away, and my office faced the railroad tracks. Do you want to know how many times a day those trains went by? About every half hour. Do you know how much noise they make? Have you ever tried to carry on a phone conversation when train is going by fifty feet away from you? You have to tell the person you are conversing with to "hold on a minute, there's a train going by just outside the window and I can't hear you." I had a lot of phone calls, too. Oh yes, one other thing: you almost had to hang on to the chair you were sitting in because the whole building "shook, rattled, and rolled" as the trains went by. One time the building *really* shook when there was a major train derailment just a few hundred feet from our building. Railroad cars were not only derailed, some were on their side. Some were even on top of each other. It was a real mess.

Speaking of trains, since I was new to the job I was in training for the first few months; there was a lot to learn. I had the book learning part of it. Now I had to put all I learned into practice.

My responsibilities were to work with all farmers and supporting agricultural businesses in the county. There were many different types of farms, including dairy, livestock, vegetable, fruit, forage crops, and poultry farmers, as well as greenhouse, landscape, and florist businesses. I also had responsibilities in cooperating and working with agricultural businesses, including bankers, feed, seed, fertilizer, farm machinery, and equipment dealers — and private farm consultants.

You will learn later about my pushing Cornell for regional Extension Specialists to work with specific audiences, covering a multi-county area.

Three weeks into my job, Frank, who was my boss and head County Agricultural Agent, told me I had to do a live half-hour TV program at an Albany, New York, station. "Holy shit!" I said. (That's my favorite expletive.) "I *can't* do that." Heard that before?

Frank said, "You can and you will." Sounds like my father!

Frederick L. Brueck

I had to write instructions for the producer and director for the audio and visual parts of my presentation, as well as for the camera shots and the whole ball of wax. I never had training in any of this.

The Saturday morning of my presentation I woke up with one hell of a headache and kept thinking, "I can't do this. I'll make a fool of myself."

When I got to the studio and got set up before the two TV cameras, I broke out into a sweat; my hands were freezing, my stomach was upset, my mouth was dry, and my headache developed into an excruciating migraine. I began to think I was going to faint.

Just as one of the cameramen was giving me a visual hand count down to go on the air, I said to myself, "I *can* and I will do this." And I did! A month later, Cornell sent out their monthly newsletter, which all Cooperative Extension Offices get, and there was something about my TV presentation. I got a 5 star rating! That was a huge boost for my self-confidence, and it gave me the will to be the best I could be.

I worked with Frank for about a year and then he left for a foreign service job in Tipai, Formosa.

Later that year, in 1959, Jack was hired as Frank's replacement. Whenever one has to work with a new person there is a little anxiety about how well you are going to be able to get along. Another uncertainty is, will I have to change any of my job responsibilities, especially the ones I like doing? Well, there was a transition period for both of us. But we became not just co-workers, but friends. Some forty-five years later we still are the best of friends.

With limited office space and with our desks right next to each other — and facing each other — we had to make some changes. We had to share the same telephone. If someone came into the office and wanted to discuss something that was confidential it became rather awkward. So Jack built a partition between our two desks. A hole was cut in the bottom of the panel so we could share the telephone by sliding it back and forth through the hole. Talk about ingenuity!

One of the big events we worked on was a "Hay Day." I guess everyone has their hay day, but this was a big event where we got a cooperating farmer to allow us to have a farm equipment demonstration field day. We contacted and got several dozen farm machinery dealers to demonstrate, in the field, their hay harvesting equipment. As each piece of equipment was operated, we announced over loud speakers the characteristics of each. Over 1,000 farmers attended! This was repeated when I moved to Schoharie County in 1961 and we had over 1,000 farmers attend that event. Farmers like equipment, especially new equipment. Some have hundreds of thousands of dollars invested in machinery. Quite often that is their downfall and they go out of business.

CHAPTER 12

MY FIRST FARM VISITS

Frank, my boss, made sure that I got out into the field and made contact with farmers and ag business people. Good grief, Frank, we have over 1,000 farmers in the county!

On my first farm call, I walked up to the door of the farmhouse. A lady, with a very red face and neck, wearing a zippered sweater, came to the door and invited me in. I introduced myself and said I was looking for her husband. "Oh, he's very busy out in the field." I said, "Well, I won't bother him. So how are you?" She said, "Better than I was." I said, "Why, what happened?" She replied, "I was pressure canning tomatoes, and the top of the pressure canner blew up and I was scalded from my face to my navel." She unzipped her sweater and said, "Look." Boy, did I look. No bra! I just stared at 2 big "fried eggs". "Oh, my", I said and got out of there in a hurry. Now what will happen on my second farm visit?

Believe it or not, on my second farm call, I went into a barn and was greeted by a very unhappy dog. He walked toward me with his upper lip curled, his fangs showing and he bit me on the left hand as I held my clipboard out in self-defense. No farmer was around so I went to the house. A lady came to the door and asked, "Can I help you?" I said, "Yes, did your dog have a rabies shot lately?" She said, "Oh no! not another dog bite." Her daughter, who was a nurse, came to the door asked what happened, then went back in and came back

73

out with a swab of alcohol and bandages. The dog had had his rabies shot. And he had just taken a pretty good shot at me. I had a puncture wound in my hand but I did not have any complications from that episode.

This reminds me of one of my favorite *Pink Panther* movies, where Peter Sellers, as Inspector Clouseau, walks into a small hotel in Switzerland. A little old man smoking a pipe is behind the reception desk. Next to Sellers is a dog lying on the floor. Sellers asks, "Does your dog bite?" The old man responds, "No, my dog doesn't bite." So Sellers bends down to pet the dog and the dog bites him on the hand. Sellers says, "You said your dog doesn't bite. He just bit me." And the old man says, "That's not my dog."

By the end of my thirty-three-year career I had twelve episodes where a farm dog attacked and bit me. Shouldn't I have gotten some kind of medal for bravery or service above and beyond the call of duty?

Several months went by and one day, after arriving home to the "box," I was going through the mail and one envelope got my attention. In the upper left corner it said Selective Service System. Immediately I knew this would not be good news. It wasn't. In effect, the message was for me to be at the bus stop on Main Street in Johnstown to board a bus that would transport me to the Veterans Hospital in Albany. After arriving I had to go through the army physical. Now, you know that when you have a physical with your doctor, it is one-on-one. You know: you are in the privacy of the examination room. Not so with the army. I had to stand with at least thirty other scared guys, all lined up in a row and totally in the buff. (If you don't know what "in the buff" means, it means even your socks are off.) A team of doctors goes down the line checking everyone out. One sticks a thermometer in your mouth. (At least it was in the mouth! Do I have to explain that one too?) They check everything, including grabbing your private parts and squeezing the things that squirrels eat. I thought I would go nuts after that episode. Anyway, after the torture was over, I handed a letter to one of the doctors that looked like he knew what he was doing. Then I boarded the bus to go home. The letter was an old one I kept from the time I had a series of X-rays of my back when I was a kid to find out why I always had back pain. It explained that I had Spina Bifida in my lower back and a rotated spine in my neck and upper back. A month later I got a letter from the Selective Service System stating that I was declared 4F: unfit for military duty. If I had been drafted I don't know how I would have been able to pay my bills, especially the mortgage on the "box." But I would have served my country if I had to and would have found a way to pay my debts. That would have been an easy one: the spouse would have to pay off the house!

CHAPTER 13
TRAVELING CHEAPLY

One day my wife said to me, "don't you think it's time for *us* to travel?" "OK, where do you want to go?" "Across the country." "What? We can't afford that. We can't stay at motels, it's too expensive." "Camp out!" "No. Who wants to camp out in the rain?" "You're pretty good at solving problems and thinking up things. So think." I did. Here was the solution:

I bought my third car on bid and purchased a four-door Ford. First I took the back seat out, then opened the trunk. Between the trunk and the back seat there was a steel "web" for support for the back seat. Using a hacksaw, I sawed the top and the bottom of both sides of the steel webbing and bent them back. Now, measuring the distance, I sawed a 4' x 8' sheet of ¾ inch plywood so it would fit through the trunk up to the front seat - with the front seat moved fully forward. On top of that platform, I put a double sleeping bag with two air mattresses. Finally, to keep out tiny bugs and flies, I bought some very fine aluminum window screening. This was cut to fit the front and rear windows and it was attached to the inside door frame with, what else, but duct tape! My wife made some curtains and we pinned them to the underside of the roof, which at that time, was made of cloth. Underneath the "bed" there was room for a camping stove, freezer chest, extra clothes and boots, emergency medical kit, and various other essentials. Now we had a motel on wheels.

Farmers always used to call me the "idea guy." But thanks to Pop, there are no such words as "I can't do it."

Now that we had the travel bug, we took my vacation time to visit the National Parks of the western United States. At that time, Mission 66 was in full progress. It was a federally sponsored program to improve deteriorated and dangerous conditions in the National Parks, the result of a massive visitor boom after World War II. It was to be completed in 1966. New visitor centers with clean bathrooms and improved camp grounds were built. You could buy a National Park Golden Eagle pass for ten dollars and get into all of the National Parks. What a deal.

We visited a dozen Parks including my favorites: Yellowstone, Bryce, and Zion. When you travel, as we did, you need to find pit stops and grocery stores. That was no problem. If we were in between two parks, separated by a long drive, and we were tired, we could pull off the road where it was safe and call it a day.

You really need to be cautious about parking in outlying areas or in the boonies. Once, we pulled about one hundred feet off the road, and parked on some sand dunes. We were in the desert areas of the Southwest. We went to sleep in our "home on wheels" and in the middle of a very dark night, the ground started shaking and there was a long loud noise that sounded like a train. It was a train. We had parked ten feet away from the Santa Fe Railroad! Another time, we pulled off the road and went up a paved roadway and parked off the road. At 5:00 am, we heard a truck slow down and stop. I parted the curtains and there was a dozen men dressed in the strangest white with black striped uniforms. We had parked inside the Utah State Prison. So if you are a traveler, be aware of your surroundings.

I hope you have taken the time to travel; it can be very exciting, educational and broadening, especially if you eat too much.

CHAPTER 14

BACK TO SCHOOL

In my professional career with Cornell, with time, a Bachelor's Degree was not enough. A Master's Degree was going to be required or you were out of the system. My wife had been interested in getting an advanced degree so we decided we'd better do it. In 1966, I requested and got 10 months sabbatical leave. Wait. You can't get a Masters Degree in ten months! Maybe not. But we both did it. And that included my having to write a thesis. The only stumbling block about the thesis was you had to develop a hypothesis and prove that hypothesis by statistical analysis. Yikes! That means math. I hated math. And I have to take statistics? I can't ever pass statistics. No way. Well, I really studied hard. Our graduate school class involved forty-five Extension Agents from all over the country. They had to take statistics too. Remember Pop? There's no such word as "can't"? On our final statistics exam, the class average for the final prelim was 50. I got 100!

Thanks, Pop, wherever you are. I finished my thesis, had it typed, bound and printed. What a relief!

One of the courses that was unique, and the most practical, was with Professor Carl. It was called Extension Education and while it was overseen by "Prof. Carl," each of us — all forty-five of us — had to teach a one-hour class. This was one of the hardest assignments because you had to present, in one hour, a program that you carried out in your county that was very successful. And you had to present it to your peers. At the end of the course, after the presentation, we had to have a one-hour's evaluation with Prof. Carl on how well we did and how you ranked with your classmates. That was your final grade. When it came my turn, Prof. Carl sat down with me, and using a bar graph he showed how I ranked with the rest of the class. I remember before he discussed this he said, "I wish all the others were as easy as this one." Like the statistics class, which I thought I would never be able to pass, I got the highest grade in the Extension Education class!

Here's the moral of this story. Never give up. Try again. Work hard at the task at hand. Do not get discouraged. Be the best you can be and it will open doors for you that you never dreamed were possible.

CHAPTER 15

THE NEAR DEATH EXPERIENCE

We had one week after graduation before we had to head home. Since we were in the Western states, and near some beautiful National Parks, we decided to visit several of them. One in particular seemed fascinating: Arches National Monument near Moab, Utah.

This National Park preserves over 2,000 natural sandstone arches as well as a variety of unique geological formations. In addition to the arches, there are balanced rock formations and pinnacles all with contrasting colors, landforms, and textures. It is truly unique. All these arches were created millions of years ago by water undercutting layers of the sandstone and eventually cutting a hole through the rock, thus creating an arch.

Moab, at that time, was a one motel, gas station, and diner settlement. And the motel, diner, and gas station were one building, if I remember correctly. It was a long way to get to the Park; it was uphill on a dirt road with lots of twists and turns. There were no guard rails anywhere. I would estimate that the drop offs were five hundred feet down! Half way up the mountain it started to rain. Then as we got to the higher elevations it was snowing. The road was getting muddy and the rear wheels were spinning as we fish tailed up the road. Remember, in those days all cars were rear wheel drive.

When we got to Arches the sun was out and we spent about six hours exploring and taking photos. About one hour before sunset, and tired from a lot of hiking, we started back down. On the way down where it had been snowing and raining, the dirt road had turned to mud. Other people had made the trip down before us so now the mud had ruts in it, some quite deep. As we proceeded, the mud became slippery and I got into one of the ruts. I tried to turn to the left to get out of the rut, got out of it, then started to slide to the left. Suddenly I hit the brakes because we were headed for one of those drop-offs with no guard rails. And then it happened. The front wheels of the car went over the edge and we slid about a foot more with the bottom frame of the car resting on the edge of the drop-off. Then we could feel the car slowly moving forward. Then it stopped and it began to teeter ever so slightly. We both were screaming at the top of our lungs and crying. I said, "We're going to die if we don't do something quick!" We could not get the front doors open so I said, "Let's carefully climb over the front seat and get out through the back doors." As we started to climb over the seat, the car shifted maybe a couple of inches and the whole car became a see-saw, moving ever so slightly up and down. We were right at the fulcrum — the point of balance. We made it out safely but totally drained. Now what? We got out some cookies and a quart of milk from the freezer from under the "bed" and started walking down that muddy road, not realizing it was many miles to Moab. After walking for an hour and getting tired, with darkness approaching, we really started to get scared. Could there be coyotes or even mountain lions around here? What do we do now? As we deliberated, we heard what sounded like a jeep way in the distance. It was a jeep and it was coming down the hill! Our "hero" stopped and said, "Going my way?" We got in and when we arrived at Moab; after a very grateful "thank you," we got a room at the motel and collapsed.

The next morning I walked to the garage. They had a tow truck and the driver and I went to rescue the car. We went up the same road up through the twists and turns, the ups and downs. As we were going down a hill through the switchbacks, I thought we were going too fast. I turned to him and said, "We're going too fast." He was as white as snow. I said, "Are you Ok?" He said, "No."

"What's wrong?" I asked. He said in a trembling voice, "We lost our brakes!" I'm sure my face must have turned the same color as his. I said, "Then downshift!" He said, "I can't!" (Where have you heard that statement before?) "If I miss a gear we're dead!" Now we were taking the inside turns on the left side of the road. If someone was coming our way, we would all be dead. I said, "You steer and I'll use the hand brake." This was an old truck and the hand emergency brake had a handle on a shaft attached to the floor of the truck. By squeezing the top of the handle and pulling it back, you could slow the truck down. He said, "No, let me do it, so I have a feel for when I should engage and disengage it." He used the hand brake and we were able to slow down enough to stay in the right lane. Soon we started going up the hill again and when we slowed down enough to be able to stop, we turned around, and went back down the hill in low gear to get back to Moab.

When we got back to the garage, he put the truck on a lift, repaired the brakes, and we headed back up the hill to fetch the car.

As we were going up the hill we noticed that area of the road was still very muddy. When we arrived at the car, he backed the truck up and maneuvered it so we were in line with it. He attached the winch cable to the back axle of the car and engaged the winch.

Unfortunately, instead of the car coming back towards the truck, the truck was going backwards towards the car. Guess what he said, besides the expletives? "We can't do it." For the first time, I disagreed and said, "Yes, we can. See those tree limbs on the ground over there? Let's take them and put them behind all four wheels. It might hold the truck in place." He said, "It can't work." I got the limbs, put them behind all four of the truck tires, kicked them in as hard as I could, and told him to engage the winch. The truck started to go backwards and then the tree limbs took hold and the car, making a lot of scraping noises, was slowly winched back to the truck.

We drove back to town all the way in second gear. There was no major damage to the car so the next day we headed for home, thankful to be alive. We had enough thrills in one National Park. We can go back out west another time.

There are a lot of challenges in life. Some can be pretty darn scary. If you get into a difficult situation, stop and think. What can you do you do to resolve the problem? Make a plan. Consider the options. Consider the pros and cons. Then make your decision, and hope the hell it works!

CHAPTER 16

SPECIALIZATION

In 1961, there was a job opening in Schoharie County, New York, which is adjacent to Montgomery County. At that time there were three Agricultural Extension Agents in Schoharie County, but two were leaving to go into ag business professions. That meant one person would be hired to replace the two agents. I can't replace two people, I thought. Guess what? I did. I interviewed for the job with five other candidates and I was hired.

Now there were two agents in the Agricultural Division: Stewart, who was the Agricultural Division Leader, and me. My new position was a challenge, but there was a greater challenge ahead.

After a year of working together, Stewart went on sabbatical leave for a year to earn his Master's Degree. When he came back, he didn't stay long. He got a new job as a Regional Extension Specialist in Community Resource Development in Southwestern New York State.

Wonderful! Now I've got to do the work of three people? I can't ever accomplish that feat. Maybe I should resign and do something else, I thought. Well, I stayed and did my best, working six days a week with three to four night meetings a week. This was beginning to take its toll on me.

Around this same time, Cornell was investigating regional specialization. Instead of handling a dozen programs as an Extension

Agent, it might be possible to become a Regional Extension Specialist, like Stewart's new job, and to cover a multi-county area but have several major disciplines. That sounded good to me and I pushed the University hard to go through with it.

In 1967, Cornell decided to have a "trial program" and it would be in my area of the state. It would be a four county position. I worked in two of the four counties, Montgomery and Schoharie Counties. There was another plus: Fulton County was the third county and I lived there in Johnstown for several years. Schenectady County was the fourth county and had far less farms. It was nonetheless important, though, because there were many florists, nurseries, and greenhouse operators. (And while they would not be my clients, they are considered to be part of agriculture.) I decided to apply for the position.

One week before the interview, which was to be held at Cornell, I woke up in the morning feeling absolutely horrible. I went to the refrigerator to get a glass of orange juice to quench my thirst. I took one swallow and it felt like two knives were stabbing both sides of my neck just under my ears. I ran into the bathroom, looked into the mirror and saw a chipmunk with a mouthful of nuts in his cheeks staring back at me. My neck was swollen to twice its normal size and "my nuts" hurt. Holy shit! I've got the mumps! I called my doctor. He said, "Stay in bed, lie flat on your back, just get up to go to the bathroom and to get something to eat. Stay in bed for seven days." WHAT? Seven days? I have to interview for that job in six days.

Now, here's a real dilemma: Do you stay home and miss the interview or risk your health and apply for the job?

On the sixth day, I felt better, but not that great. I went for the interview. Seven candidates were gathered in the hallway in Warren Hall on campus waiting to be interviewed. There were no chairs around. My "private parts" were really hurting now and I was fearful that I would not be able to go through with this torture. I toughed it out.

I was the last person to go into the room where four professors were waiting to grill me. It was truly one of the most painful and exhausting experiences of my life. Guess what? I got the job! I became the first Regional Extension Dairy and Field Crops Specialist hired in New York State. Several months later, my former co-worker, Jack, who had been up for the same job, applied for the second position. He got the job. His major disciplines were Farm Business Management and Agricultural Engineering. Now we were back together again. Instead of trying to cover the waterfront like I was doing, I now was responsible for two major disciplines, Dairy Science and Field Crops. We worked together until he retired in 1983.

I was very fortunate to have Jack as a co-worker. We worked well as a team. We both had a sense of humor and that made our work that much more enjoyable. We were not just co-workers, we were the best of friends and today I consider Jack and his wife Kitty, to be among my most cherished friends.

From 1983 until I retired in 1991 I worked with three different younger, but very capable, Extension co-workers. None of them lasted very long and they all went on to higher paying jobs in ag business. One of them was David. I consider him and his wife Nancy, to also be my cherished friends.

CHAPTER 17

THE FRUSTRATIONS OF BUILDING A HOUSE

When my wife and I arrived back home, having completed graduate school, we had to get used to living in the "box" again. We had a fairly large apartment when we were at Colorado State University and coming back to our mobile home was depressing.

Now that we both had a Master's Degree there wasn't any question that, with time, we would both have a higher joint income. As a result, maybe we could afford to buy a plot of land and build a real home.

Having thought about that prospect, my thoughts turned negative again. I've been in debt all of my life; I can't go further in debt now. Suppose we had an economic recession and our economy hit the skids. Or even worse, we could have another Depression. My parents went through that and it wasn't easy.

OK, I thought, there are a lot of risks in life. But I have to look more at the positive side of life. This "I can't" philosophy is never going to get me anywhere. A turtle never gets anywhere unless he sticks his neck out. The more I thought about it, the more encouraged I got. But I still was worried about getting over my head in debt.

So I went through my typical analytical thought process looking at the pros and cons:

I know quite a lot about building construction. I did take five engineering courses when I was at Cornell. I do know how to read building plans. I do know that if you build any building where you try to cut costs and skimp on the essentials, like the foundation, side walls and roof, it will eventually lead to higher costs in repairs. It has to be built to stand the test of time.

On the other hand, having a well-constructed house is going to cost more. Yes, but it will also have a higher resale value if I had to sell it. Houses usually appreciate with time. And if the plot of land I bought had some positive things about it, like an attractive setting with a nice view and a good water supply, that would be a big plus. It would also be a good idea to buy enough land so I could protect myself from getting hemmed in too closely by potential new neighbors. That would be a disaster, having lived on a farm with our nearest neighbor one half mile away.

What would happen if I did a lot of the work myself? No, I can't do that. It would affect my job and I wouldn't want that to happen.

All of these thoughts were going through my mind; I tried to sort out both the positive and the negative considerations in making the big decision to build a house. We discussed it and we both decided to go for it.

I knew what I wanted and my wife agreed. We wanted a Swiss chalet style home with a south facing exposure to capture the solar heat during the winter time. That could save on the heating bill.

That also meant a lot of thermopane glass windows. We wanted a front and side deck, a nice stone fireplace upstairs and a wood stove downstairs. The living room, and dining room would be combined so there would be one large room. I think that idea was a result of living in the "box." The kitchen would have the typical triangle, meaning the kitchen sink, electric stove, and refrigerator form a triangle. It greatly increases kitchen chore efficiency because the appliances are more closely spaced and that eliminates a lot of walking back and forth.

There were many more "we want's" but it was time to start looking for some ideas. One could drive around the countryside looking at houses, but I decided to look in magazines. It didn't take long to find something we both liked. Actually it was an ad showing a Swiss style chalet with a deck. Unfortunately it was a small vacation cabin. But I liked the design.

We also wanted both an upstairs and downstairs bathroom, and of course a two-car garage. Do you know of many people that park their cars in a garage? How come it quickly becomes the family storage area and the cars are relegated to the great outdoors?

Combining the ideas we had and the floor plan of the vacation cabin I thought we could work something out. I contacted an architect for some help and we soon wound up with a set of building plans.

The next step was to find a good contractor. After contacting several, I found the one I wanted. But there were two problems. He mainly built commercial buildings and the house plans were a challenge to him.

One night we met at his home and talked about all the things we wanted. The list of "we want's" was excessive and so was the price. He added up everything and presented me with his estimate. Using my favorite expletive, I said, "Holy shit! I can't possibly afford that. Now I'll never get out of debt." We had to do something so I decided to see if I could get a reasonable deal with a bank. But before going to the bank I made a deal with the contractor and he said he would build our dream home.

There was a small bank in town at which I had kept an account for a number of years. I knew most of the members of the Board of Directors. I contacted them, twisted a few arms, and, after considerable deliberation, I got a loan and we were ready to build.

When living in the country, before you build, you need a well for water. That's a deep subject and an expensive one. But if you don't strike water on your building lot, you don't build. Obviously, the deeper you drill the greater the cost. I found out that most of the wells in the area were drilled 400 to 600 feet deep before striking water. That is expensive.

The next decision was whether to get a well rig that pounded the well hole or a rotary rig that drilled it. Everyone I talked to said don't get a rotary rig — they can drill past the water. Nevertheless, I decided on the rotary rig because it is usually faster.

Now where do we put the house?

I knew where I wanted the house site: 400 feet from the road and up a steep hill. The drilling contractor arrived but the hill was so steep he could not get the rig up the hill. My contractor had his bulldozer sitting nearby and it was used to push the rig to the site. I didn't have a clue where to drill the well so I took a twig from a tree, pushed it into the ground and said, "drill here." This was 7:30 in the morning. I left for work at 7:45. At noon, I took some time off to see how the crew was doing. To my dismay, the rig tower was down and I thought they haven't even started yet. I went up the hill and asked what happened. They said, "We're done…we got 12 gallons per minute at 67 feet." I replied, "Holy shit! are you kidding me?" It was true. Most folks around here are lucky to get one to three gallons per minute. So I lucked out again.

I had another problem. The site where the house was to be built was wooded. Most of the trees were soft wood, white pine, and red cedar. I had oak and maple trees nearby but they were far enough away so they were not a problem. How am I going to cut the trees down? The simplest answer was to buy a chain saw. My typical answer was I can't afford to buy one. So I cut the trees down Paul Bunyan style, with an axe! In a later chapter I will tell you all about felling trees. That means how you cut a tree down so it falls in the direction you want it to go and doesn't land on top of you. I had one fall on me! Once the trees were cut down they had to go somewhere. There were two choices: Use the contractor's bulldozer and push them out of the way, or I could cut them into fireplace size logs and split them for cozy wood fires in the fireplace. Since I had an axe and a bow saw I could do the job myself. It took a lot of time and energy but I got the job done.

But wait. What about the tree stumps? The simplest answer was to have the contractor push them out with the bulldozer. But that would leave a lot of ruts to fill in because that area was going to be my backyard. So what did I do? I had a pick axe and shovel so I dug around the stumps and kept chopping the roots with the axe until I was able to push them over. They were small enough so that I could push them away with my new walk behind Graveley garden tractor that had an attached four-foot-wide snow/dirt blade. I had bought it for plowing the snow off the driveway.

The next challenge was the driveway. I got all kinds of advice but it boiled down to either putting in switchbacks or going straight up the hill, which would be the shortest distance between two points. We went straight up the hill. I needed a parking area for cars so we had to use the bulldozer to cut into the hillside, and then had to cut and fill until the area was level enough for the house site.

Now we had a level area, but we left a cut into the hillside which, if left alone, would most likely erode and possibly cause a mini landslide. That meant a retaining wall. Holy shit! I can't afford to have the contractor put in a retaining wall. Hey, I could do it myself! But how? Here's an idea: I have a stream that runs along the boundary of my property. There are tons of stones and rocks of all sizes and shapes. Many of them are flat. So I could build the stone retaining wall myself. Wait! How am I going to get the rocks up the hill? It was about four hundred feet up that steep hillside. I can't do it! Impossible! Think a minute. What can I do? I asked some of the workers if they knew of somebody that had an old beat up four wheel drive pickup truck for sale. My plumber said he had an old beat up army Jeep. How much? $50. Sold! I worked for months after work but I got the stone retaining wall built. It still stands there to this day. I was 36 years old at the time and loved physical work. Boy did I get a work out. But by determination and stupidity we had the site ready for building our dream home.

The building crew, although they had a lot of challenges, proceeded fairly well. But it took much longer than the contractor figured on. He told us we should be able to move in sometime in November. When December came, I said, "You said November." His answer, "I didn't say what year!" We moved in on December 7,

1967, Pearl Harbor Day. I got bombed that night in celebration of our first day in our highly mortgaged new home.

The bottom line of this chapter is life is full of challenges. Some good. Some bad. You have to decide whether you are up to the challenge. No one said life would be easy. And I had the will to keep trying, despite the odds. How are you doing with the challenges in your life?

CHAPTER 18

THE SCHOLARSHIP TOUR

Yes, another tour. In 1968, I had the opportunity to join twelve Extension Agents from a dozen different states on a three-week tour of the eastern United States. This was a Dow Study Scholarship Tour, sponsored by the Dow Chemical Company. It was a whirlwind trip I will never forget.

Of course, I had to go through that you-know-what problem I had. "Golly, what an opportunity. But I can't do it. I've got too much work to do." But I decided it would benefit me professionally and, accordingly, it could benefit my clients. We would be visiting the best of the best farms and businesses. I would also be privileged to go to some places that were off limits to the general public. And so I embarked on another adventure. The tour visited nine states: Pennsylvania, Ohio, Illinois, Indiana, Maryland, Virginia, Kentucky, Tennessee and North Carolina. We visited marketing enterprises, outstanding farm operations, resource development projects and research and demonstration trials. It was the research and demonstration trials that drew my interest.

One of the unique ideas of this tour was you had a different roommate each night. Too bad it was an all man tour! We swapped ideas and talked about our different programs including our successes and failures. That, in and of itself, was worth the trip.

We had the opportunity to visit Fort Detrick, Maryland, about a one-hour drive from Washington, D.C. It was, at that time, a top secret government agency that carried on all kinds of experiments, some you wouldn't want to know about.

We had a tour of Gasoline Alley at the Indianapolis Speedway. Only race car drivers and their pit crews are admitted there. But being VIP's, we got in. At the time we were there, Hollywood was filming a movie titled *Winning* with Paul Newman and Robert Wagner. Race car driver A.J. Foyt was there for the technical part of the movie. We visited for a moment with Wagner but the fun part was watching Paul Newman. Short scenes are done repeatedly until they get a "take". Then the combined scenes become a movie. We watched a scene that was shot at least a dozen times. Newman was supposed to open the door of a convertible car, throw his suit jacket over the passenger seat, get in the car and start it. That was it. They had a problem. Each time they tried to film the scene the car wouldn't start. They must have tried a dozen times. It makes you appreciate what goes into the production of a movie.

There is usually a clown on most trips who tells stories and likes to joke a lot. One of the guys, Jim, was always cracking jokes. We were at a restaurant where an attractive lady was playing the piano. He walked up to her and wanted to know if she knew how to play the upright organ. (Sorry about that.) Then there was "Farty Frank." We all had the unfortunate opportunity to be his roommate and we compared notes. One night he would be constipated, so he'd take a laxative. The next night he was up half the night going to the john. Then it was back to constipation. Well, you get the drift!

One stop that got my attention was near Hopkinsville, Kentucky. Here the local Extension Agents were conducting research trials on no-till corn. What is no-till corn? Traditionally, when planting corn, the soil is plowed, then it is broken up with a disc or a drag to prepare the soil. The disc chops up the plowed furrows and the drag further prepares and levels the soil. This involves several trips over the same field before planting the corn with another machine called, what else, but a corn planter.

The Extension Agents, with the cooperation of the Allis Chalmers Farm Machinery Company, were planting corn with a new type of planter that had a fluted coulter on the front of the planter that cut and prepared a narrow strip of soil. The corn seeds, in hoppers on the planter, were dropped in that narrow tilled strip and a packer wheel behind the seed hoppers closed the slot and firmed the soil.

So what's the big deal? It involved only one trip over the field instead of two or three. If corn was planted on a hay field, a chemical herbicide was sprayed to kill the vegetation and then the field was no-till planted. Time is money and extra trips over the field cost money in higher fuel and higher labor costs.

A while after I got back from the trip I conducted similar demonstration trials on twelve farms in two of the four counties I covered. I also conducted similar no-till perennial forage demonstration trials on other farms. I was asked by Extension Agents and ag businesses across New York State to make slide presentations at farm meetings about this revolutionary way of planting crops. One meeting in Central New York drew 400 farmers; a second meeting in Western New York had 600 in attendance. That year I was awarded a National Association of County Agricultural Agents Distinguished Service Award (sponsored by Ciba-Geigy, an international chemical company) for bringing this new technology to New York State.

I know this is a bit technical for you but I thought that you might be interested in the fact that agriculture, and farmers in particular, are always looking for cutting-edge technology to find ways to increase their efficiency and at the same time keep costs down. Remember, agriculture is the largest single industry in the United States. Without the farmer, where would your food come from? Grocery stores do not grow the food. Farmers do.

CHAPTER 19

LISTEN TO YOUR DOCTOR — KICK THE HABIT

Shortly after building my house, Mom and Pop came up for a rare visit in December, 1969. As Pop walked off to have a cigarette, Mom started to cry. "What's wrong, Mom?" She said, "I think your dad has throat cancer."

He did. He was a three-pack-a-day smoker. Mom smoked one pack a day. This habit was started long before Sis and I were born. As a child through adulthood, Sis, with severe asthma, had to inhale that smoke. She always complained about it and it definitely aggravated her asthma. Parents, as well as other family members who are smokers, need to consider the rest of the family, especially when smoking indoors and especially with someone around who has breathing problems, like asthma.

As a result of his smoking and the onset of throat cancer, Pop had to have an operation to be able to feed himself through a tube in his throat. The doctor said to him and I quote: "Start up smoking again and you'll be dead in six months." After that warning, when convalescing in the hospital and later at home, he stopped smoking. Maybe he had a death wish or perhaps he really couldn't kick the habit, but he started smoking again. Six months later he died of lung cancer. Mom said it was an agonizing way to go. I wonder if they ever thought about their smoking habits, especially with a daughter with severe asthma. To make matters worse, most of the time they smoked in the house.

I had to live in that situation as well; I became sensitized to cigarette smoke at an early age also. No, I never got asthma, thank God. But to this day, some thirty four years later, if anyone lights up, especially indoors, I get a coughing spell that doesn't want to quit.

In my opinion, smoking in public places, like restaurants, or wherever people gather, is a selfish habit. Yes, there are smoke free restaurants, but what about the bar in the restaurant or any other public place for that matter? If one has to smoke, go outside and get your nicotine fix.

Better still, get help and kick the habit. You might enjoy life more and you just might save your life. Kicking the habit is probably one of the hardest things anyone has to face. I know of many friends who smoked, and through pure will power they were able to stop smoking and never smoked again. Others I know have repeatedly tried to stop and they failed every time. And, like Pop, in their failure to stop, they faced an agonizing death.

CHAPTER 20

THE HARDEST DECISION OF MY LIFE

Several years after my father's death, Mom had a stroke. Sis had been taking care of her but she could not handle it. After a short time, Mom had to be put in a nursing home. Shortly after that she had a series of "strokes showers" and had to be hospitalized. Then came a call from Sis. "You better come to the hospital. Mom's not very good."

Karen, my second wife, as explained in chapter 27, and I took the four-hundred-mile round trip drive to the hospital in Rochester. When we walked into the room, I couldn't believe my eyes. Mom was writhing back and forth, black and blue all or over her body from having to be tied down. She had her eyes closed and was babbling like a baby. She was being tube fed. After a few minutes, a doctor walked in the room. I asked, "How long has she got?" "Not long," he said. Right then, Father Fred, the family priest, walked in. He was making his usual hospital rounds, visiting and comforting some of the members of his parish. I turned to Father Fred and said, "What should we do?" He said, "It's OK, tell the doctor to remove the feeding tubes and let her go." In the old days of the Catholic Church, that was a no-no. I talked to the doctor and she died shortly after that wrenching decision I had to make. Goodbye, Mom, I loved you.

I wish I had expressed that more often when she was alive! This is one of the lessons of life. Wishing I had expressed my feelings doesn't count. What does make a difference is expressing your feelings often and meaning it when your loved ones are near and dear to you. I failed in that count.

CHAPTER 21

CATS AND THE VISIT

CATS was a winner on Broadway. Sis was eventually a loser when it came to cats.

When I was in college, Pop and Mom sold the farm and moved into a nice rambling ranch house. They had a nice large yard with woods on one side and farmland behind the backyard.

Sis continued to live with Mom and Pop when they made the move. She loved animals and began to take in stray cats. She started with one, then two. The numbers kept going up and when she died there were twenty-two cats in the house.

Now that's a lot of cat litter — and a lot of "you know what" to empty every day. But she didn't empty the litter boxes that often. So now you had to watch where you walked.

I looked forward to seeing Sis on the rare visits we made. But walking into that house was like walking into a rotten garbage dump; it was a horrible situation. The cats spared nothing. Curtains were torn to shreds, all the furniture became scratching posts, and sheets of newspapers were all over the floor to soak up the urine. And Sis wasn't doing too well. Obviously, the cats were not helping.

Sis was born on Memorial Day. Several years after Mom died, on a Memorial Day, Karen and I went to visit Sis. Before leaving home, I loaded my roto-tiller and a new lawn mower on my truck. The lawn mower was her birthday present.

When we pulled into the driveway, the manicured lawn I was used to seeing had turned into a hay field. The grass hadn't been mowed all spring.

We greeted Sis, wished her a Happy Birthday and we talked for awhile. She really didn't look good.

I unloaded the mower and tiller. Karen started mowing the "hayfield" while I started to till the garden. Sis sat in a lawn chair watching me work. After a time, I needed a break and sat down next to her.

I asked her if she was OK. As usual, she said, "I'm OK." I said, "I don't think you are. What's wrong? You can tell me. After all, I'm your brother." She said, "Oh, nothing's wrong." On the third attempt, she said, "Oh, I discovered a lump on my left breast." What? I asked her when she had discovered it. "Oh, a couple of months ago." I asked, "What did the doctor say?" "Oh, I haven't been to see a doctor." I told her, in no uncertain terms, "You either call the doctor tomorrow or check into the emergency room of the hospital. I'll call you tomorrow night." After I finished tilling and planting her garden and Karen finished mowing the lawn, we said goodbye and headed for home.

The next night I called her. "What did the doctor say?" "Oh, I didn't call!" This went on for over a month. Finally I drove all the way to Rochester again for a talk. She told me her breast had numerous small lumps and the nipple was oozing puss. My heart sank. I knew instantly that she wasn't going to make it.

When she finally contacted a doctor, he told her "she was a goner." She was in denial, and suffered for a very long time. The cancer had spread to her bones and throughout her body. She died a horrible death six months later.

Ladies, if there is anything you get out of this book, please remember the title, Never Say Can't. Sis couldn't make the call because she was fearful of the results. It cost her her life! Get an annual mammogram. Examine your breasts monthly. If you don't want to examine your breasts, ask your husband or boyfriend to do so. You might enjoy it! And it could save your life! By the way. MEN CAN GET BREAST CANCER TOO. So men, you know you have breasts with nipples. Yours just aren't as nice or large or as soft, or as attractive as a women's. But that doesn't let you off the hook. You need to examine your breasts for any lumps. Let your wife or girl friend show you the technique. It might tickle a little but, like I said before in this chapter, it might just spare you from dying from that horrible disease.

I know all about the ravages of cancer. My father's mother, my grandmother, died of stomach cancer. You just read about my father. His sister, my aunt, had breast cancer in her fifties and she told her doctor, "Cut em off!" That saved her life. I saw her when she celebrated her ninety-first birthday. Soon after her birthday, the cancer returned. She never complained of any discomfort or pain. One day she went upstairs to her room and never woke up. She was the lucky one. Even though she had cancer, she was spared all the pain and suffering, both mental and physical.

One final thought: The only way we are going to be able to spare perhaps you, or your loved ones, from this dreaded disease is through research. How about doing what I have been doing for years? Support your local chapter of the American Cancer Society.

CHAPTER 22

CLEANING UP THE MESS

After Sis died there were four things that had to be done; I wasn't looking forward to any of them. First, I had to take care of the cats. Second, I had to clean up the house. Third, I had to find an attorney. Finally, I had to find a buyer for the house.

Since I am an animal lover, I had to find a way to rid the house of the cats. There is no way that I would contact an exterminator. That would have been the easy way out. So what should I do? How about contacting Sis's veterinarian? I made the call and explained the situation. I mentioned that Sis had spent thousands of dollars on those cats and most of that money went to him to pay the vet bills. I asked if he could help me out. Could we trap the cats with Havaheart traps and take the captured cats to his clinic or the animal shelter for adoption? I had a Havaheart trap that I had used to capture raccoons in my garden. After they are caught, I take them a distance away and release them. These traps do not catch an animal by a foot with steel jaws; it is simply a large cage with a treddle in the center. The treddle looks similar to a child's teeter-totter. The cage is baited with cat food. A cat walks in and eventually steps on the treddle. That causes the two ends of the cage that are hinged at the top to drop down. The animal is safely captured.

After three weeks of trapping, twenty-one of the twenty-two cats had been caught. One escaped out the garage door when it was opened. Hopefully it found a new home.

The veterinarian had a girlfriend that lived about twenty miles away. She was also a veterinarian. Together, through their clinics, they found homes for the twenty-one cats. What a happy ending to a horrible nightmare!

Now for the rest of the nightmare: How do I clean up the house? The first step was to dispose of just about everything. I was able to get three of the largest dumpsters available. Then the fun began. Where do I start? The first thing was to toss out all the furniture, lamps, tattered curtains, beds, kitchen table and chairs and anything else that would fit in the dumpsters.

Next step: Go through every drawer in the house. There could be something valuable somewhere. After a while I was overwhelmed with making decisions on what to keep for myself and what to toss out. There wasn't much to keep. I found some of my sister's jewelry. Nothing expensive but it could go in a yard sale. I found several photo albums that reeked of cat urine, but there was a lot of nostalgia there so I kept them. One of the sad things I found in the hall closet was a glass syringe with a three inch long rusty needle. Next to it was an empty bottle with a label that read adrenalin sulfate. This was proof that Mom did have to give Sis adrenalin shots to keep her heart stimulated until the ambulance arrived.

One day, while all the cleanup work was proceeding, there was a knock at the door. A man wanted to know if the house was for sale. Was this a miracle or what? I spent a lot of sleepless nights wondering and worrying about how to get rid of the house. Who would want it? Wait until they get inside the house. I invited him in but warned him about the mess and the smell.

After a thorough tour he said that the house had potential. I thought, for what? He explained that he was a contractor and that it could be repaired. All the walls and floors would have to be replaced. The wall needed to be insulated, covered with sheet rock and painted. The outside of the house was attractive and there was a large yard. He made me an offer. Luckily I found an old appraisal of the property in a safe deposit box that my parents had in a local bank. Of course I never found a key to it so I had to pay the bank $100 to have it drilled open. His offer was for half of the appraised value. I took the offer and that ended one of the worst experiences of my life.

Meanwhile I had to have a yard sale. I never had one and I never went to one. Karen was a huge help in working with me sorting through all the trash in the house. A big plus was she loved to go to yard sales. Wow kid, have I got a job for you!

I put a number of ads in the newspapers advertising the time and date of the sale. Lucky for us I found some saw horses to block the driveway. It was supposed to start at 9:00 am on a Saturday. People were lining up around 7:45 and I thought I might have to call the cops for crowd control. After the sale, I vowed I'd never go through another yard sale. It's a good way to clean up the clutter and junk. (As the saying goes, "one person's junk is another person's treasure." We cleared over a thousand dollars from the sale of all that "junk." In later years, I did have two garage sales to get rid of some of my "junk."

There was another thing I had to do: contact an attorney for all the legal necessities to settle the estate. I retained my parent's attorney. It had taken Karen about three years to get her parents' estate settled; I wasn't going to wait that long.

The attorney wanted to do a bank search; I told him, "I already did that." He said he would take care of paying all the bills. I said, "No, I'll take care of that." He had a lot more things he said he would do, and I said, "All I need from you are the legal papers necessary for selling the property." In three weeks I had everything done. All I had to do now was make one more trip to Rochester to sign the papers. When I got there he called his staff into his office and said, "This is Fred, the guy that did most of the legal work." They all clapped their hands, and I signed all the documents and headed for home with a big sigh of relief.

Behind the Iron Curtain

By Frederick L. Brueck

This fascinating first person account of an agricultural leaders' visit to Europe, highlighted by a tour of Russia, was written by Extension Specialist Frederick L. Brueck on the request of The Times-Journal.

* * *

FREDERICK L. BRUECK

CHAPTER 23

BEHIND THE IRON CURTAIN

In 1972, I received a call from the head of the research department at a major agricultural cooperative. He was leading a delegation of farmers and agricultural business representatives to the Soviet Union. It was a people-to-people tour, a concept started by President Eisenhower to stimulate better relations between the former U.S.S.R., now the Soviet Union, and the United States. People in this country met with their counterparts overseas.

My first thought was "I can't do that. I don't have the money to pay for it. And I can't take the time off from my job." But then I convinced myself that this was a great opportunity. There's nothing like turning what you think is a problem into an opportunity.

115

This was not your typical tourist trip. We were in a country where former Soviet President Kruschev, pounding his shoe on a table, on live television, said to the people of the United States, "We will bury you!"

The Soviet Union is a vast country. The United States, Great Britain, Germany, France, Italy and Japan could easily fit within its borders with room to spare.

The people of the Soviet Union are as diverse as the country, with over 100 nationalities. Its resources are enormous.

Before entering the Soviet Union we were briefed by our department of state on the dos and don'ts when traveling within the country. We were told that every American who travels in the Soviet Union is subject to Soviet laws, regulations and restrictions. These laws are often very different from our own and are strictly enforced. Persons violating Soviet law, even unknowingly, run serious risk of arrest, trial, fine, and even imprisonment. Knowing this and hearing about all the stories about the Soviet Union over the years gave me a sick sensation in my stomach. Did I make a mistake in going on this trip? No. It was well worth it.

Our adventure began with our arrival in Moscow. The first thing we noticed was the foul smell in all the public buildings. We could not decide whether it was clogged sewers or just plain decaying garbage. We later discovered that the putrid odor emanated from the disinfectant and soap used for cleaning the buildings. Their toilet tissue is not much better. It came in two forms — waxed paper or sand paper!

Moscow, the capital and largest city in the Soviet Union, at the time I was there, was the fifth largest city in the world. It encompassed thirty-four square miles with over seven-million people. The first thing we noticed was the thousands of apartment buildings, wide streets devoid of traffic, and vast numbers of people walking along the sidewalks. Since everything is publicly owned, there are few private homes or personally owned vehicles. Only the high officials and socially elite own cars. Most of the traffic consisted of buses taxis and trucks. The most common means of transportation was either walking or taking the subway.

The Kremlin by the Moscow River

Riding on the Moscow subway was a unique experience. It was one of the most efficient and beautiful subways in the world. Stalin-era mosaics and chandeliers decorated the ceiling. The walls and floors were marble. It was always crowded, but it ran on time.

We visited the Exhibition of Economic Achievement in Moscow. Housed in temples like pavilions, the 100,000 different displays ranged from the largest sputniks to laying hens; from computers to farm machinery. At the time we were there, the exhibition proved that their technology was as advanced as ours. However, their equipment lacked the quality found in the U.S.

A tour inside the Kremlin in Moscow will not soon be forgotten. The Kremlin is the embodiment of Russian culture. The Kremlin walls enclose towers, cathedrals, palaces and government buildings, erected from the fifteenth to the nineteenth centuries. It is a concentration of Russian art, architecture and history.

We visited the Cathedrals of the Assumption and the Annunciation. They contained many magnificent icons and decorations. Religion was not completely banned but it was discouraged to the point where most of the worship was done in secret. One Sunday we wanted to attend a church service. Our Soviet guide gave us the typical Russian response to anything that had not been arranged or preplanned for us: "nyet." That means no. When asked why not, the typical answer is, "That is impossible." Through sheer persistence we were able to attend a Russian Orthodox service.

The inside of the church was beautifully decorated with gold leaf on the walls and ceilings but it was sad to see so few people in attendance and most of them very old.

While religion is discouraged, the arts are encouraged. We had an opportunity to see the world famous Russian Ballet at the famous Bolshoi Theater. It enjoys tremendous esteem in Russia, and rightly so: It has produced some of the world's best dancers.

My most vivid and lasting impression of Moscow was in Red Square at night. It was directly adjacent to the Kremlin, and was a Russian landmark. It was the site of the imposing Lenin Mausoleum. Thousands of people gathered to watch the changing of the guard at Lenin's tomb. Saint Basil's Cathedral was a beautiful scene at night with flood lights concentrated on the different shapes and colors of its bulbous domes. I started to take pictures with my camera and a young Russian couple approached me shouting, "nyet! nyet!" After several minutes of drawing pictures on a piece of paper, I concluded that one should photograph the cathedral only during the day time. That made no sense to me. During the course of our "conversation" I noticed a rather stern looking man observing us. At least three other times I noticed this same man following me. Later I learned he was one of their KGB or secret police. We were warned never to take photos of structures like bridges because you could be arrested for perhaps planning to blow up that bridge at some future time. Does that sound familiar? Today we face terrorist attacks around the world.

Since part of the purpose of this trip was to study agriculture in their country, we visited a number of farms. At the time of our trip there were two kinds of farms: state and collective. State farms employed a director appointed by the government. Collective farms also employed a director, but he was elected by the members of the collective farm. On state farms there was no sharing of any profits, but on collective farms the members received incentives and share in any profit. I don't need to tell you which of the two types of farms was the most successful. Their farms are very large. We spent one day visiting the Kropotkin State farm in Kresnadar near the Black Sea. It was a very large diversified farm that employed over 1600 workers. Now that is big time farming! But their animal and crop production was far below that of the United States.

Prior to leaving, we had a dinner with representatives of the farm. I can't remember what we ate but I can tell you what we drank: Beer, wine and vodka. And did we ever drink. First they raised a shot glass and saluted us. We did the same to them. Then it was the same thing all over except it was wine. This was followed by beer while we ate dinner. I don't have to tell you that all of us had one hell of a hangover the next morning as we prepared to leave for home.

I remember Don, a member of our group, was sitting next to me in the airport waiting for our flight announcement. All of a sudden we both started to get stomach cramps. We decided we better find the bathrooms pronto. Suddenly we realized we could not read any of the signs. I said let's just follow the people walking ahead of us and if someone goes into a doorway with signs over it we may be in luck. We were in luck but there were no doors on any of the toilet stalls. There were no toilet seats either. There was only a concrete pipe and you had to squat over it. I felt like shouting "bombs away!" Then there was newspaper, but it wasn't for reading. The final insult was an old woman with a broom. She looked like she should use it to take off on runway 22! Her job was to take care of "your job"! It seems that some people missed the pipe. Boy were we glad to get the hell out of there and board our plane for the long flight home.

A discussion about the Soviet Union would not be complete without reminding you that this trip was in 1972. Things have changed. Back then they believed that private enterprise was ineffective and that genuine progress could be obtained only when the interests of the individual coincided with those of a planned society. Be proud that we, as Americans, live in freedom and that only the productive are strong and only the strong are free. Oh, I almost forgot. Mom got her money back six months later. Thanks, Mom.

If there is any message that I can pass on to you, it is appreciate the freedom you have. It's priceless.

CHAPTER 24
THE SHERIFF COMETH

In 1972, I had the opportunity to attend a five-day seminar at the Chicago Mercantile Exchange to study grain future's trading. I was encouraged by Cornell to go because grain farmers could monetarily benefit by hedging in the future's market. It is much too complicated to discuss fully here, but here are the nuts and bolts:

A future's contract is an obligation, a legally binding agreement, between a buyer and seller of a commodity, like corn or wheat, to receive or deliver that corn or wheat some time in the future but at a price agreed upon today. You are essentially gambling about what the price will be in the future. You can make money or lose your shirt. I would rather go to the casino and play the slot machines.

Why did I go? We had some very large farms in the counties I covered. In the 50's we had a farmer, who, by the way, was a fellow Cornellian, who grew several thousand acres of corn and received the Ford Foundation Efficiency Award for producing 180 bushels of corn per acre on 450 of those 2000 acres. That was, at the time, a yield that a farmer could only dream of achieving. We had a very large family in another county I worked in that grew eight thousand acres of corn. That beats the pants off many of the farmers in our midwestern corn belt states.

When I got home from the Chicago trip I entered the house and there was the obvious smell of cigar smoke. (I've got the nose of a bloodhound.) I greeted my wife and asked, "Who was here smoking cigars in the house?" When I was a kid my parent's house smelled of cigarette smoke. To me cigar smoke is a lot worse. Her answer: "Nobody was here."

My suspicions were confirmed by a few close friends. I wasn't the only man in her life! I was dumbfounded.

Then one day when I happened to be home early from work and there was a knock on the door. There stood the sheriff and he handed me an envelope. I said, "What's this?" He said, "I don't know, it's addressed to you." I was used to our mail lady. But the sheriff? We argued a bit, but I took the envelope, went upstairs, opened it, and surprise-surprise. It was a letter from an attorney. In essence, my wife was filing for divorce. What the ____ is going on?!

She wasn't kidding. Not only did she get the divorce, she got half of the appraised value of "our" home and property. To prove that "I wasn't the only man in her life," she built a home, with some of my hard earned money, and had an open house to show it off. Some dear friends of mine went to her open house. They asked me why my ex had mirrors on the bedroom ceiling! I left that to their imagination.

I lived alone in my own highly mortgaged dream home for the next eight years.

CHAPTER 25

FLYING HIGH

After the divorce, I directed most of my efforts and time to my job. I always worked a sixty hour week that included, on average, three night meetings a week. That is not necessarily a healthy thing to do. Some of my friends encouraged me to go out more. Socialize and have some fun. Make new friends. Get involved. Take some courses. It took some time for their advice to sink in.

About five miles from my home is a two-year State University of New York Agricultural and Technical College. I was on three of their advisory boards for a period of time and I knew mini courses were offered to the general public. Following my friend's advice, I decided these mini courses were something I could so that I could get out and about.

My first course was all about golf. Now I never could figure this game out. What is so much fun about hitting a little white ball as hard and as far as you can to get it into a hole in the ground? And after many tries with a hand-held device called a golf club, after you still can't get that stupid ball in the hole, you fling the club as far as you can, shouting expletives and profanities. I don't get it. And why do they call it a golf club? Maybe it's because golfers club the ground in frustration. And if they get that frustrated, why do they even attempt to play the game? Is this really a game? Chess or cards are games. Maybe it should be called a golf challenge.

The first time I teed off, I took a mighty swing and missed the ball. On the second swing I threw my back out. I should have thrown the golf club and quit right there. I tried several more times and that was it; no more golf. Years later, I found myself golfing twice at William Holden's Mount Kenya Safari Club on two different trips to Kenya, Africa. I did not do any better attempting to hit that stupid ball in Kenya but it was much more interesting with storks, peacocks, and a number of strange animals walking the golf course with you. (You will read more about Kenya in Chapter 24.)

Tennis was next on my list of fun things to do. Here's another game or sport or whatever you call it that seems stupid.

Again the goal is to hit a ball, this time much bigger than that little golf ball, and to hit it with a hand-held device called a racket. I understand the strings were once made from cat intestines. Now I'm a lover of cats, and I find it repulsive to try to hit a ball with the remains of a dead cat!

Well, at least I tried it but I found it was a pain. It was a pain in my elbow that lasted almost three months. My doctor said it was tennis elbow. It takes a doctor to discover that?

The next mini course was a come on. And I really did come on to the tune of tens of thousands of dollars over a twenty year period. It was titled: Learn to Fly!

It was really an introduction to flight dynamics — i.e., how does this machine manage to stay in the air? It does have wings and an engine but there's got to be more to it than that. So here is my interpretation of what the instructor took six weeks to teach:

There are four forces acting on any airplane, whether it is a Piper Cub or a 747 Jumbo Jet. They are lift, an upward force; gravity, a downward force; thrust, a forward force; and drag, which is anything that can slow the plane down, like rivets on the "skin" of the plane or wheels that are not retractable.

So how can a plane stay in the air? Lift has to exceed gravity and thrust has to exceed drag. Got that? OK, let me try again.

On the front of a small plane, besides the engine, is a propeller, otherwise known as the prop. The blade of the prop is shaped like a small airplane wing. The blade has a twist to it that provides an "angle of attack." The prop is like a revolving wing. Low pressure is formed in front of the prop, resulting in thrust. On the big birds, the jet engine provides the thrust.

But here's the real secret: if you look closely at an airplane wing, it is flat on the bottom and curved on the top. As you start down the runway to take off, the air takes longer to go over the curved top of the wing than it does to go along the flat bottom of the wing. This creates a negative pressure on the top of the wing and a positive pressure on the bottom of the wing. This is what gives you the lift to get the plane into the air and keeps it flying.

The key now is to keep those engines running. If they stop in midair it's called a panic attack.

One of the nice things about the course was a free plane ride. That's referred to as an incentive to take flying lessons.

When I was a kid I used to make stick and paper model airplanes. It can take weeks of after school time to put one together. I also carved airplanes out of balsa wood. So I really was interested in flying at an early age. And so I took a plane ride.

You've heard about "Hooked on Phonics" for kids? Well, this is called "Hooked on Flying for Adults."

My instructor was really good, but he was a real grouch. If he told you to do something you better get it right the first time. If you goofed, you'd get an earful like, "Are your eyes open?" or "What the hell did you do that for!"

It takes, on average, about 50 hours of instruction with you flying the plane and the instructor shouting in your ear before you solo. Solo means you are up there in the sky all by your lonesome saying Hail Mary's.

I'll never forget my first solo flight. But first, I have to tell you about the airport. The airport was right next to our local college. It had an 1800 foot airstrip at an elevation of 1200 feet. The hills around the airport are about 1600 feet in elevation. An 1800 foot strip is short but okay for a small plane — a very small plane. Why?

At this particular airport, on the east end of the runway, there were three very tall elm trees. If you were coming in for a landing and were lucky enough to clear the trees, your next obstacle, beyond the trees, was a barbed wire fence running perpendicular to the runway. The fence was to keep the college's cows in the pasture and off the runway. By the way, they used to have cow catchers on the front of train locomotives! Did you know that? If so, you are about as old as I am. Speaking of trains, on the west-side of the runway, running parallel to it and about 20 feet away, were the D & H Railroad tracks. On the east side of the runway was a very long hangar where you kept the airplanes. Finally, at the west end of the runway, the worst hazard was a twenty-foot drop off. This drop off was created when the highway department put in a new road to make a shortcut to another road. I know a lot of pilots that went off the end of the runway, including my family doctor.

So now I hope you get the picture. This was a very dangerous place to fly in and out of. There were lots of accidents.

I got to solo after about 40 hours. I made an appointment for a Saturday morning. The only problem was we had an ice storm on Friday. When I got to the airport, the runway was a sheet of ice. But it was a bright sunny day. Wow! The sun was a real confidence booster. At least, it wasn't foggy. Now they don't tell you when you are going to solo. If they did you may not show up because of fear!

On that bright Saturday morning, I got in the left seat. That is always the pilot's seat. My instructor was in the right seat or co-pilot's seat. I took off and did some takeoffs and landings, partly to test the icy conditions. We stopped with runway to spare. After the third landing, the instructor told me to taxi to the end of the runway again. We turned around, he opened the door, stepped out and said, "good luck" and slammed the door. Yikes, I guess that meant I was ready to solo. But take off and land on ice? It is comforting to have an instructor to take over if you goofed. Now I was on my own, but I didn't say, "I can't do this on this icy runway." My brain was trying to convince me to taxi to the hangar and try another day — like in the spring. My heart was racing faster than the engine. But I bit the bullet and took off. I flew around for a while, mainly because I feared landing on that icy strip. Coming back to land I kept saying to myself, "Come on Freddie, you can do it." I made a perfect three point landing. It must have been all that concentration. I taxied to our little building, a short distance from the runway. There were toilets there as well as coffee. I guess the coffee is why they have the toilets. Actually I think the toilets are for student pilots who have to throw up either before or after their first solo flight. Nobody told me what comes next. My instructor came up behind me, pulled up my coat, shirt and undershirt, and ripped the shirt off my back. Then he took a pen and wrote: Fred Brueck soloed January 9, 1969. That was a real high. Again, no pun intended. The moral of this chapter: flying gave me a big boost in self-confidence. I could do it. If I could fly an airplane, I could do just about anything. Well, not really.

You can do what seems like a big challenge to you just as well as I did. You just keep trying until you get it right. Never say "I can't." In my case, I just keep flying until I get it right.

the author's solo flight

CHAPTER 26

WATCH YOUR STEP

Around the same time I was flying around the countryside, I got caught up again by another "come on".

I was reading the Sunday paper and saw an ad: Free Dancing Lesson. Here we go again! Oh, what the heck. If it's free, I don't have to go back after that first lesson. So I said (well, you know what), "I can't dance. I've got two left feet." Then I thought more positively. Maybe this might be an opportunity to meet some nice lady. I'll give it a try.

This was a first-class dance studio and the dress code for men was suit or sport jacket with tie. No tails. But afterwards, you could go out and have a "couple of cocktails to relax."

My instructor was Jean, a very nice, tall, slim, attractive lady. A nice start, wouldn't you say? Unfortunately for her, my very first step was on her big toe! Why do lady dance instructors have to wear high heels? They should be issued combat boots for klutzes like me!

I really enjoyed it and looked forward to the next lesson. It was like a free date. But, what a price to pay for those "dates"! Tally it up and I spent over $1000.

We started out with the fox trot. Now, why do they call it the fox trot? I have an over population of foxes that have dens in my woods. I see them frequently. They don't trot. Horses trot. I also learned the waltz, samba, tango, mambo, mambo-jumbo (Ok, there's no such thing) and disco.

It is amazing how complicated ballroom dancing can be. There are many different turns and steps you need to learn for each type of dance.

Here is an example, rather complicated, about all the possible combinations of steps in the fox trot. You have the magic step, magic left turn, magic right turn, left box turn, right box turn, conversation promenade, promenade walk, chasses (side steps), single twinkle, swing step, magic left quick turn, box step, swing step, two turn, magic steps turning, magic left one-half turn, magic step in parallel, corkscrew in single twinkle, society tempo, and the list goes on. Guess what? This is just for the fox trot!

Here is a minor point, but it can make a major difference for a dancing couple: ladies, remember that the man leads. Some women try to do the leading. Here's a tip: the man's right arm is held out perpendicular to his body. The lady's left arm rests on top of the man's right arm. Their two arms are basically locked together. So if a man steps forward, and if his partner concentrates on that "arm lock," she will know to step backward. If he turns to the left, she will sense she has to follow into that turn. And so it goes. It is a simple principle but very important on the dance floor.

What does learning about how to dance have to do with writing this book? It was not only a confidence booster, it helped me realize that you can be the best you can be if you try. Never say "I can't." I didn't give up. Several weeks before completing the manuscript for this book, I found a letter in my desk drawer from Jean. In it she said I was the best student she had ever had. If that's true, it was because I really tried hard to concentrate on what she was instructing me to do and I practiced those dance steps at home alone, pretending I was dancing with some beautiful women. Well, I can dream, can't I? That was the title of a song many years ago.

CHAPTER 27

THE SECOND TIME AROUND

There was a farmer in my county that had a large dairy farm and he called me fairly often for advice. He was also a fellow pilot and owned a Mooney 231 with retractable landing gear and all kinds of avionics, including radar. I got to fly it once. It cruised at 230 miles per hour, almost twice the speed of my plane.

On occasion, he would tell me about this very nice teacher at a school several miles from the farm. All his kids had her in school and all the kids respected and loved her. And she loved to teach mathematics. WHAT! Math? That was one of my worst subjects. He kept saying, "You really ought to meet her." I said, "Nice try, Jim, but no thanks."

A short time later, I got a call from Jim's wife. She said, "We're having a Christmas party in our farm shop with food and we have hired a band for dancing. It starts at 8:00 pm. Be there!" Then she hung up. I thought nice going Irene. Why don't you tell it to me straight instead of beating around the bush. Ha, I thought. Fat chance.

Then I thought about it. Maybe this nice school teacher might be invited too. So, instead of saying, "I can't" I decided what the heck. I'll give it a try.

Would this be another fatal mistake? Stay tuned. When I arrived there, right on time, I looked around and everyone was paired up. No single lady. After sweating for 20 minutes, Jim's wife called me over and said, "Fred, I'd like to introduce you to Karen. She's our local math teacher." After some small talk, the band started to play. "Would you like to dance?" I asked. "Sure," she said. We danced until 2:00 am! Thank God for those $1000 dancing lessons. I asked her if I could drive her home. She said, "Sure." She said sure a lot. Maybe I'd get lucky! We sat in my car at her home for an hour, talking about traveling and all the trips we each had taken. At least we had something in common. Finally, I asked her if she would like to come to my home to see some slides of a few trips that I took. That's like saying, "Would you like to see my etchings!" So we decided a time and date, I bid her good night and headed for home. In 1980 we got married. I left out the "goodies" for your imagination!

CHAPTER 28

TRAVELING AROUND THE WORLD

Before Karen and I got married, she had traveled to a number of European countries. Most of my travels centered around the National Parks and National Monuments in the United States. Any overseas travel was business related, like my trip to the Soviet Union.

I also traveled to Sweden and Denmark via a Cornell Cooperative Extension Dairy Tour, hosted by Extension agents in Columbia and Dutchess Counties in Southeastern New York State.

My first impression of Sweden was that all the women were blond. Second, all the women were gorgeous, and third, all the women had beautifully sculptured bodies. I didn't see much of the countryside because I spent so much of my time looking at those beautiful bodies, including those that were nude on the beach.

Most of the tour involved visits to farms and research stations. I learned a lot about their farming practices and some of their ideas were passed on to some of my farmer clients when I got back.

After Karen and I were married, our first trip together was in the United States but far from the mainland. We visited four of the Hawaiian Islands with another couple who were mutual friends of ours. We flew from island to island, rented a car on each island, and saw more in ten days than most people would see on a typical bus tour in a month.

But the real adventures came when we went out of our country. I could write a book about all those experiences.

My first reaction when Karen wanted to travel overseas together was "I can't take the time off right now. I'm too busy with my job." I slowly began to realize that all work and no play not only made Fred a dull guy, but it just wasn't healthy to devote all of one's time to a career. You need time off to learn, explore, and have fun. And so what follows are some of the highlights of travels to over thirty five countries from 1980 to 1996.

We had both been to England, Scotland and Wales before, but we wanted something different than a typical bus tour. Karen wanted to do the ABC's: another bloody church, another bloody castle, and another bloody cathedral.

We began by looking through my many National Geographic magazines and their accompanying maps of the three countries. One of the fascinating things my father had told me, when he was sober, was that someone had traced our ancestry to a count in King Arthur's Court. My first reaction was, I don't believe there really was a King Arthur. It's just a fable. We did find a description of the ruins of King Arthur's Castle in one of the magazines. That convinced me. We were going!

When we got to the site that was documented on a National Geographic map, we did find the ruins of a castle on the edge of a cliff. But there was not much to see except the remains of a foundation. What I do remember was the "castle" hotel we stayed in near the ruins. It was a huge stone building with extraordinarily large rooms. A little old lady greeted us. I was not sure whether she was a ghost or a real person, the way she looked! The only memory I have now is how cold it was in our room. Also, when you walked to the bathroom at night you heard the echo of your footsteps on the stone floor. Ghosts? I don't think so but we were glad to get out of there.

One of the really funny but sometimes frightening parts of the trip was renting a car and trying to learn how to drive all over again.

As you know, you drive on the left side of the road in these countries. But if you haven't done this before, you quickly find out that the driver sits in the right-hand seat. We had a standard shift transmission. Since we are both left handed, you would think we would get used to it. I wound up driving the whole trip. Karen got vertigo from sitting in the right seat, shifting with her left hand, and having the rear view mirror cocked in the "wrong" direction.

Several times we almost got killed by stepping off a curb to cross a street with cars coming right at us because they were driving on the left side of the road. We looked the wrong way first, which is fine, if you are at home.

Another interesting experience was the "roundabouts." If you want to make a turn onto another road, you have to go around a circular roadway to get to that road. The only advantage I see to this is that if you miss the turnoff (you can't back up), you can keep going around the circle until you get off at the right road. It takes getting used to driving in these countries, but wait until you get back home.

On the drive back home from Kennedy airport, I almost made the mistake of driving on the left side of the road when leaving the parking lot.

I have been to Germany, Austria and Switzerland five times. Why? Well, I am of German descent so these countries are fascinating to me. The scenery in all three countries is unbelievable, what with the snow-capped Alps in the background. The gorgeous chalets that are nestled at the base of the mountains, with their unique balconies and cascading geraniums and ivy dangling down, remind me of a Walt Disney fairy tale.

Karen and I drove through these three countries several times. Now, the good thing is that you drive on the right side of the road. The bad thing is that the names of the streets are so long and are in a foreign language, making it very difficult to find the road or street you want. Also, many had similar names. And the name of the street or bridge can have twenty letters in it! We did a lot of stopping to figure where the hell we were and where we wanted to go. Looking at the front cover of this book, you will note my last name is Brueck. Translated, it means "bridge" in German. In the countries of Germany, Austria and Switzerland, bridge is spelled brucke. But you can have over a dozen letters in a bridge's name, follow by brucke. Like Sloschenhovenbrucke. Be prepared if you plan to drive in any foreign country by yourself. You need a driver and a navigator.

While we were in Austria, I wanted to show Karen Schoenbrunn Palace in Vienna. I had been there twice. It is one of the many Imperial palaces in Vienna. This Baroque style Palace is set around beautiful gardens. Only 45 of the 1441 rooms were open to the public and only for guided tours. The lavish Rocco interior of the Palace was designed by Empress Maria Theresia. The palace has many state rooms. Some of the most impressive were the living quarters of Emperor Francis Joseph; the Hall of Mirrors, where six year old Mozart gave his first concert; and the Viewx Room, where Napolean met with his generals. Many of the walls and ceilings in the different rooms are gilded with gold leaf. Floors are inlaid with many different kinds of wood in spectacular designs. A fresco on one of the walls was unique. It showed a soldier on a battlefield. When you walked towards the painting and then past it, his eyes followed you! Really!

Schoenbrunn Palace

The funny thing about going to the palace was that we couldn't find it initially. We went all around the city three times before we found it. We went by it twice. How can you miss a palace with that many rooms?

Our trip to Egypt and Israel, in 1993, was bittersweet. When we arrived in Tel Aviv on the first day, we had that uncomfortable feeling that we stood out like sore thumbs. Gentiles in a Jewish country. I also had that uneasy remembrance that a few years before, scud missiles were raining down on the very place we were staying.

Arriving and departing from the airport, while scary, gave you a comfortable feeling because everyone had to go through very strict security. My video camera was confiscated and completely taken apart. Who knows? Even back then someone might have had a similar video camera that was wired to blow plane and its passengers into oblivion. Back then, video cameras were bulky and you shot scenes with the camera resting on your shoulder.

Israel is truly a religious experience. Its history goes back more than 2000 years. We followed in the footsteps where Jesus walked when we were in Bethlehem and Jerusalem, from his birthplace to the exact spot where he died on the cross. We took a boat ride on the Sea of Galilee, which was inspirational, in spite of the many other tourists on the boat.

When we were near Capharnaum, our guide showed us a site where it was believed one of Jesus' disciples had lived. Because of the ever shifting desert sands, one site can be buried under dozens of feet of sand, while another find could be exposed by those same winds. Digging down about ten feet they found the remains of a house. There was a name inscribed on one of the crumbling walls. The name? Jesus. Awesome!

While much of Israel was inspirational, it was also scary at times. We had just completed the Way of the Cross, traversing the steps where Jesus carried the cross to his crucifixion, and we were warned that walking among the crowds of people were many pick pockets. As we proceeded down a crowded street there was a huge explosion. You could feel the concussion. Immediately our guide said, "Look straight ahead, walk fast, but don't run." We never knew what happened. Despite our fears it was well worth visiting this small but fascinating country.

Egypt is also a fascinating country. When you see pictures of the pyramids at Giza, near Cairo, they look impressive. When you stand beside one and see individual stones weighing tons, it is hard to believe how people could possibly have built these massive triangular structures that are the tombs of kings. There are many theories but we still don't know how they managed to build them.

Seeing all the treasures of King Tut in the museum in Cairo is beyond belief. Much of what we saw was made of solid gold. As a matter fact, most of the treasures on display in the museum were made of gold. It would take you several days to really see everything.

Equally impressive were the tombs in the Valley of the Kings. When we arrived in the desert it was 122 degrees Fahrenheit in the shade! In that heat and very low humidity, you do not realize how easily you can become dehydrated. We always carried a bottle of water with us to make sure we stayed hydrated. Even then, if you brushed your hand along your arm you could feel the crystallized salt from perspiration.

Going down a long flight of newly built concrete steps took us into several chambers where the kings were buried. There were hand painted murals in vivid colors on the walls and ceilings. The amazing part of this was that these paintings looked so bright it was like they were freshly painted. They were painted 5000 years ago! But sadly, with increasing tourism, the murals are starting to fade. Why? Carbon dioxide! We breathe in oxygen but exhale carbon dioxide. And it's the carbon dioxide that is causing the paintings to fade and thus, threatening to close the tombs to tourists to preserve these magnificent treasures.

One day, while in the office, my secretary said, "There's a call for you, Fred, from Kansas." Kansas? I cover four counties in eastern New York State. They tell me I'm good at what I do, but I didn't realize I was that good!

The person calling said, "Have I got a deal for you." I replied, "Thanks, but no thanks." I thought it was another salesman selling a new brand of widgets. He exclaimed, "Please, don't hang up. Let me explain. I represent XYZ Travel [name changed to protect the innocent] and you and your wife can get a free trip, all expenses paid. All you need to do is get at least 20 people to sign up." I threatened to hang up and he said, "I'll give you the names of several of your counterparts. Call them. Ask them about our company." I called Jessie and Larry, whom I respected, and they gave me the details. Both said it was a great opportunity. Don't pass it up. Thus began the opportunity of a lifetime.

I have always been very conscientious and would never let this interfere with my job. At a Board of Directors meeting, I asked if I could host a tour using my vacation time and said in no way would it interfere or be tied to my job. And I would never use our mailing list or use my job as a "come-on."

They voted unanimously that, using my vacation time, I could take one trip a year. And so we did.

Our groups averaged about twenty people. Over the years about 200 people took these tours, which covered Brazil, Argentina and Chile in South America; Australia and New Zealand; Sweden, Norway and Denmark; Germany, Austria and Switzerland; England, Scotland and Wales; and Kenya, Africa. These were repeat countries for us but it was nice, for a change, to "travel by bus and leave the driving to us," or so the motto goes.

Nevertheless, even when traveling with respected tour companies with excellent drivers and tour managers, there can be challenges for a tour host.

On the first tour to England, Scotland and Wales, our tour manager approached me early in the morning with a major problem. There was another group from the Midwest that was supposed to join our group. On the day of their flight out, there was severe weather around O'Hare Airport in Chicago and all flights were cancelled. They were to fly to Heathrow Airport where our tour guide was to meet them the next morning. Our combined group was to tour the Tower of London that day. Now here's the problem. Our tour guide said to me, "You are going to lead your group to tour the Tower of London while I meet the Midwest group at Heathrow Airport." My favorite expletive comes next. "Holy shit! I can't possibly do that. This is one of the biggest cities in the world. I get lost in Albany, the capitol of New York State. Besides, it's your job, not mine." He said, "The Tower of London was a big part of this trip. The people paid for it and they are going to get their money's worth. Here are the tickets. A double-decker bus will pick your group up here. Gotta leave now. Good luck!" As this conversation was going on, I began getting one of those horrible migraine headaches, with an upset stomach and flashing lights in my eyes. No way can I do it now. Karen came over and said, "You can do it; we can't let our people down." I agreed and, despite my desperation, I led the group on the tour. When we got on the bus we went to the upper deck of those famous red double-decker buses. Everybody started singing and laughing. That lifted my spirits and everyone had a good time on that tour. Even me!

This is one of many examples where I was confronted with a task that was unexpected; where I felt very uncomfortable, figuring I would get everybody lost and it would turn into a disaster. It turned out to be a fun day.

I hope you will think about the times you had a task to do and you felt it was too much to handle, only to find out you did the job and did it well. Remember those occurrences and learn from them. You can do it. Be confident in yourself.

CHAPTER 29

THE THRILL OF A LIFETIME

zebras in pinstripes

The best, most interesting, and adventuresome trips we ever took were our two Kenya, Africa, safaris. Our first safari was with a tour company out of New York City. The second trip was with the "XYZ Travel" company I mentioned earlier. I was the tour host of this trip, as was true of all the tours we hosted with this company, and Karen was the tour hostess. This chapter offers you some of the highlights of both trips.

When you go to a zoo, you are free to walk around and see the animals in a cage or in a confined area. On safari, *you* are in the "cage." In most cases the "cage" is a van with a pop up roof that allows you to stand up when the van is stopped. This provides for much better views and much better opportunities for taking photos or

151

panoramic views with a video camera. The animals are free to roam throughout their territory. You aren't.

I'll never forget Joanne. She had never traveled before and really wanted to go but was hesitant. Africa is a long way from home. She bit the bullet and joined our group. Her family was at the airport to say goodbye and on return they were there to welcome her home.

We were in a van near a waterhole, where many species of wildlife came to drink. In the distance there was a knoll and suddenly a huge elephant, the matriarch or "boss," followed by about a dozen other elephants came into view. They were heading our way. Tears began rolling down Joanne's cheeks as she saw the "parade of the elephants." They stopped at the waterhole about a dozen feet away. It was totally awesome! If you ever felt insignificant this was the time; we felt like ants.

Elephants are a marvel. They can use their head and powerful legs to uproot large trees. And yet they can pluck a single leaf off a tree with their trunk. I suppose if I weighed six tons, I might be able to push a small tree over. They always travel in small herds with the dominant female, or matriarch, leading the way. Bulls are solitary.

Cheetahs are members of the cat family. They are much smaller than the lion. They have beautiful spotted fur coats and unfortunately, in the past, they have been killed so women could wear their fur coats. They are a thrill to see, especially when you are 20 feet away and watching their cubs playfully chasing each other. They are the fastest animals on earth. They have been clocked to run in short bursts at sixty miles per hour!

The Black Mane Lion, the king of the beasts, is equally awesome but in a different way. A 600 pound male can take down and kill a wildebeest as large as a horse and kill it by either breaking the neck or by suffocation with its powerful jaws clamped like a vise around the victim's throat. Actually the female lion is more deadly than the male.

We saw a number of sad instances involving lions. There was a very thin female lion walking with two cubs following behind her. She had a large gash in her side. The gash could have come from any one of the many different species of antelope. Most species have very long, sharp horns for self defense. Our guide said it was doubtful that she would live, and if she died the cubs would die from starvation. In another situation we saw a solitary lion with a broken jaw. She was probably chasing a zebra and got kicked in the face. She would not survive either. While these episodes are very sad, it reminds one that, whether human or animal, we all have to deal with tragedies in life.

One of the lodges we stayed at was on stilts. The only way you could get in or out was via a draw bridge. It was raised at night so you could not go for a walk. Even so, no one ever goes for a walk in Africa, day or night, unless it is in a city. Even then you don't go out alone. All night long lions were nearby. Some were underneath the lodge roaring. It was probably some lioness in heat looking for some action! Some years earlier we were told that at this same lodge a doctor on safari wanted to go out for a short night walk. The management refused to allow anyone to go anywhere. But the doctor decided he was going for a walk so he went down a fire escape ladder. He never came back. He was killed by a Cape buffalo, the most dangerous of all the African animals. If they attack you, you would not have a chance to outrun them, or for that matter, most any other African animal.

The migration of the wildebeest is unbelievable. Wildebeests look something like a horse but with a goatee and horns. Actually they look like the devil. From horizon to horizon, as far as the eye can see, wildebeests travel at a specific time of the year to new grazing grounds.

We happened to be there during their annual migration. Wildebeests were backed up along the Mara River bank by the millions waiting to cross to the other side. But they were waiting for one brave soul to go first. Why? Because they have to literally jump off a cliff to get to the water. Would you jump off a fifty-foot cliff into a river that is full of crocodiles to get to the other side? All it takes is one crazy but brave wildebeest to jump. Once that first one jumps they all follow, and that is where you have a "traffic jam!" The first ones in the water can't swim fast enough to avoid the millions that are to follow. So a lot of them drown. There are dead wildebeests all along the river. Pity the poor young calves who, if they survive, have to find their mothers in this "sea of animals." Then there are the crocodiles waiting for a meal. There is plenty of "food" for all.

Monkey see, monkey do. Watch out for them! It's not uncommon for them to come up to a van, jump onto or into the van, grab a purse or camera and run off, leaving you penniless and flimflammed — no, that's "film" flammed.

Leopards are beautiful members of the cat family. Our guide told us about an episode another guide had with a group of Japanese tourists that he had in his van. They stopped to watch a leopard in a tree. Leopards sleep during the heat of the day in trees and hunt at night. Everyone was taking pictures with the pop-up roof fully extended. Suddenly the leopard stood up in the tree. The guide said, "We have to leave." One woman insisted they stay. "No" the guide said, "It's too dangerous." She insisted they stay. During this short conversation, the leopard bounded down the tree, raced towards the van, and with one leap, was inside the van. Everyone got down on the floor but the leopard had already done his damage. He tore the breast off a woman with one swipe of his paw. The guide risked his life and jumped over the seat to pull the leopard off the screaming people. He was successful and the leopard ran off. That's not the way a safari should end. But it did. The kicker: the driver was sued by the woman that insisted on staying to take more photos!

We were witnesses to a more personal tragedy. Our group was scheduled to be the first out on a game drive one morning. Our schedule was changed and a group of bird watchers from Connecticut got our time slot. Birding in Kenya? Yes. Kenya has 1054 species of birds. Some are so colorful they look like a mad artist's painting.

The Connecticut group started out at sunrise looking forward to a day of adventure. Adventure it was — of the worst kind! They were driving through the bush when Somalian army deserters, with AK47 rifles, suddenly jumped out demanding money. One woman refused to give up her purse. She was shot dead on the spot. We would have been the group assaulted if our schedule hadn't been changed! We had some unexpected circumstances on other trips but they pale in comparison to that one.

One morning we were headed for Lake Naivasha, an alkaline lake situated 6200 feet above the Rift Valley. We stopped on a bluff overlooking the valley. In the distance was a pink lake with a pink shoreline. Pink? Yes, and as you traveled closer to the lake, you realized that you were seeing over one million pink flamingos!

Hippos are often referred to as water horses. They spend a lot of their time submerged in the water eating whatever plants and grasses they can find. One could be in for a big surprise in a small boat in a river or lake if a hippo raises its head to come up for air.

Speaking of air: there is nothing like going for a balloon ride across the Serengeti Plain. I went on two different balloon rides on our two trips to Africa; Karen went on the first one but not on the second one. There was a reason why she only went once.

Going up in a hot air balloon is a real adventure. Going in a hot air balloon ride over the Serengeti Plain in Africa is an awesome adventure. Before we went for the big ride we had to get up in the wee hours of the morning, eat breakfast, then load into a van to be driven to the lift off. We had a rather large women in our group. "How large was she, Johnnie?" She was so large that she had to wear two seatbelts on the 747 trip to and from Africa. That's no joke. As a matter of fact, she couldn't get into the van. Several natives came up behind her with their hands on her backside and pushed. It took a third person, using his foot, to get her in. I sat in my van watching this and wondered how we would ever get her out of the van. When we arrived at the takeoff site she got out of the van but then we couldn't get her into the balloon. She finally got in via a step ladder. This was the world's largest balloon. In addition to a dozen canisters of propane gas, there were about a dozen of us in the basket. The gas is used as a "blow torch" directed into the bottom of the balloon to heat the air inside the balloon; that allows the balloon to slowly fill with air. Soon it slowly rises and we have lift off. There is a valve at the top of the balloon that the pilot opens and closes via a rope to gain or lose altitude. Once airborne you slowly glide over the vast plain in silence, except for the sound of the jets of flame every so often to gain altitude. You can see for miles and you pass over many of the animals I described earlier. While all of this is going on, there is a ground crew following as best they can in a four-wheel-drive vehicle. They have to go over some pretty rugged territory, and sometimes we lost sight of them but they soon caught up.

The culmination of the flight is when you touch down wherever there is a safe place to land. But that isn't the end of this adventure. Before we took off our pilot told us about the landing procedure. There was a large thick rope all the way around the inside rim of the basket. On landing, before touchdown, you were to squat down, hang on real tight to the rope and keep your head down. As we were coming down close to touch-down, there was a large termite mound that was in our path. Some of these mounds can be a dozen or more feet high. The basket hit the mound and flipped upside down. The gas canisters landed on top of some of us. The balloon was still partially inflated and the wind was dragging us along the ground. The ground crew was right behind us now and the pilot was screaming at the top of his lungs at the crew to get the basket upright. There was a possible chance that the canisters might ignite and boom; that could possibly be the end of the trip and possibly the end of us. It turned out OK, except Karen was crying and holding her hand. In all the excitement she had one hand holding the top rim of the basket and not holding on to the large rope inside the basket. So when we tipped over and were dragged, her hand got mashed. Fortunately one of the passengers on the balloon was a doctor. Her hand was only badly bruised. And now you know why she didn't go on another balloon ride when we went to Kenya a second time.

This still isn't the end of the story. Once the balloon was down and everyone was out of the basket and settled down a bit, the ground crew came over and spread out a large tarp for us to sit down on. What's going on here? It's time for breakfast! They brought us all we could eat or drink. What a thrill to be in the middle of a huge plain with wild animals roaming in the distance, having breakfast in the cool of the early morning. It was like a religious experience.

There were many adventures in all the other countries we visited, but Kenya will always be our favorite. By the way, remember those disastrous golfing lessons I took? We golfed twice in Kenya at movie actor William Holden's Mount Kenya Safari Club. I mentioned it in an earlier chapter; this was a very exclusive club. We had some of the best food I ever had in my life. Some of the dessert was molded and sculptured into the shape of many of the animals we had the privilege of seeing. We had a native come to our room at night and start a fire for us in the fireplace. When we got up early in the morning we went outside and watched the sunrise near 19,000-foot snow capped Mount Kenya, the highest mountain in Kenya. Mount Kilimanjaro was not that far away in Tanzania.

While parts of this book are about gloom and doom, with all the problems I have had to deal with, there were a lot of good times too. Kenya was the best of the best. I feel I have been privileged to be able to see such fascinating countries as Africa. As of this writing, I have been in all fifty states of the United States, all the provinces of Canada that border the U.S. and 35 foreign countries. Maybe I'll have to write another book about all of those other adventures.

CHAPTER 30
THE CHALLENGES OF BUILDING A BARN

Shortly before I decided to go into the sheep business, I needed extra storage space for a tractor and truck, small equipment and who knows what else.

As I mentioned in chapter 18, the only piece of "construction equipment" I had was a walk behind Graveley garden tractor with a four-foot blade that could be used for snow removal or moving dirt.

Everything here, at my home, is on edge. Sometimes I am too! Since most of my land is sloping, one has to have a level area for constructing anything, even a dog house. I did all of the leveling for the barn with a pick, shovel and wheelbarrow. I also had to do this for a sixty-foot long lane way from the house to the barn.

Since this was going to be a pole barn, which is a common building for storage, I had to dig 16 holes by hand. The only problem was I had to use my hand-operated post-hole digger. I thought to myself, I can't dig 16 holes, four feet deep. But once again, with determination I did it. Why is this such a big deal? To dig a four-foot hole with a hand-operated post-hole digger, you need to keep making the hole wider the deeper you go. The reason is when you take a "bite" of dirt with the blades of the digger, you need to spread the two handles apart to hold the dirt for dumping it outside the hole. To dump the dirt you push the two handles together. This was not fun because I hit shale rock in some holes and large boulders in others.

The shale and boulders had to be broken up with a heavy steel bar. Then there was the challenge of how to get the larger rocks out of a deep narrow hole. But it got done.

Next step: one needs a concrete pad at the bottom of the holes, otherwise the poles can settle and that eventually means a crooked roof. I bought bags of concrete mix, put it into the wheelbarrow, added water and used a garden hoe to mix it. Then I dumped it into the hole and tamped it down. On my hands and knees, I used a trowel and a small level to make sure the concrete in the bottom of the hole was level. One has to make sure the concrete hardens before setting the poles in the holes.

To build a pole barn, you obviously need poles. I used 6 inch by 6 inch pressure-treated creosote poles. (Creosote prevents decay.) Did you ever try to get a 6 inch by 6 inch square, twenty-two foot long pole into a three-foot diameter hole by yourself? Do you know how much each pole weighs? And once the pole is in the hole it has to be vertical and perfectly straight. They have to be braced with 2 by 4 inch pieces of lumber. That's where Karen was a big help.

The next step is to put the roof on. It was quite a task to carry up on a ladder heavy 2" by 10" pieces of rough-sawn lumber for the roof rafters, 2" by 6" pieces of rough sawn lumber for the purlins (which are nailed crosswise to the rafters) and heavy sheets of steel roofing that are nailed to the purlins. Nailing on 1" by 12" rough sawn pine board siding was a breeze. All it took was hard work, determination and stupidity for not hiring a contractor! Now I had a

36 foot wide by 60 foot long building for putting just about anything in it. It even has a loft in one part of the barn for all the extra junk one collects.

one rock that had to be broken up with a sledge hammer

CHAPTER 31

THE GOOD SHEPHERD

One day a good friend, John, asked me why I was mowing my old hay fields. He said, "Why not raise sheep and let them do the mowing for you?" His dad raised sheep and they cleaned up the weeds and kept things trimmed down and looking neat. You know what's coming next: "I can't. I have a full time job. I don't have extra time for sheep. It is going to cost a lot more than they are worth. I will have to buy hay, grain, and salt. I'll have to put up a whole fencing system to keep the sheep in and the predators, like coyotes, out. If I went on a trip, I'd have to hire someone to care for them."

I thought about his advice and despite all the disadvantages, I decided to give it a try.

So in 1982, I contacted another friend, also named John, who was a professor at our local college. He had a 200-ewe sheep flock. We visited and he sold me 12 cull ewes. Buying cull ewes is not the brightest thing to do. I should know that more than most folks. But if I decided it wasn't going to work out, I would not have much of an investment in them.

Some months after I bought the ewes I rented a ram. He bred the ewes and five months later my sheep flock went from a dozen sheep to 30 sheep. It is common for ewes to have twins and triplets.

Some have quintuplets. Over a period of time, I reached a peak of 178 ewes plus their lambs.

One of the rams I rented was named Hampiedoo. Hampiedoo did! He bred the first five sheep in twenty minutes. Wham bam, thank you, ma'am! Best of the dozen rams I rented over several decades.

Any extra time I did have, which wasn't much, was spent on caring for the flock. Feet had to be trimmed, fences built and repaired and the sheep had to be fed twice a day from late fall to the following spring. All the grain and hay had to be bought and hauled in my truck. They ate 18 tons of hay from fall to early spring.

There are some things, while requiring a lot of work and extra time, that make it all worth while, like caring for the lambs and watching them frolic around. Kittens and puppies are cute, but I think baby lambs are even cuter. One of the biggest challenges in raising sheep is at lambing time. Take delivering lambs — somebody please! Now I am not pulling the wool over your eyes when I describe the birthing process to you.

the curious triplets

The miracle of birth is always awesome, whether a human baby or a baby lamb. Humans go to hospitals. Ewes stay home and lamb in pens in the barns or in pastures. The downside is they seem to like to lamb at night when you should be sleeping. So you need an intercom in the bedroom and one in the barn. I can't talk to them. They only know ba ba. But I can listen for the ba ba. And if I hear it at night I know either they are going to have a lamb or lambs, are having them or did have them. In any case, to be the "good shepherd," you need to be with your flock under all conditions — like the time it was 22 below zero outside and 19 degrees below zero in the barn. With heat lamps over the pens, out of the 600 or so lambs I had over the years, I only lost about a dozen from hypothermia.

There are challenges, like having twins, triplets, or even quintuplets. There are a few sheep that have had six lambs! But only one lamb can come out at a time. Now, I have large hands, and trying to reach in the vagina to pull out a lamb was initially a challenge for me and certainly a challenge for the "mom." What is even worse is to have twins or triplets coming out of one ewe while three other ewe's are having contractions, meaning they are starting to lamb.

Here is a typical scenario when you have multiple births: With the "mom" starting contractions, the first thing you should see is the two front feet of the lamb coming out of the birth canal. That's front feet, not back feet; you have to know the difference. Front feet bend at the knee. Back feet don't. If there is a problem, like the ewe is straining but nothing is happening, you need to go into the birth canal, and with your hand, feel around and decide if the front feet or the back feet are going to come out first. If the back feet are coming out first, push the feet back in, turn the lamb around, grab the front feet and pull.

It's like my airplane days, flying in a fog where you can't see out. In this case, you can't see in. You need to be sure the two feet are attached to one lamb, not two feet attached to two different lambs. If you find two front feet on one lamb and start pulling, but nothing happens, you have another problem. Chances are the lamb's head is turned back. OK, so now you hold on to the front feet, making sure they are fully extended. With the other hand reach in, find the head, put your hand behind the head so it is facing forward, and pull again. In the meantime the "mom's" thinking, "What the hell's going on back there!" Even at 19 degrees below in the barn, without any heat lamps, you will be sweating.

Another typical problem is a breech birth, where the lamb is coming out backwards. Again two choices: The first choice is to reach in and turn it around then pull it out. If you decide to simply pull it out backwards and you know the two legs are from the same lamb, one must pull hard and fast. If you take your merry old time and pull slowly, the umbilical cord might break while the lamb is still inside. When this happens, the breaking of the umbilical cord sends a message to the brain signaling the lamb to start breathing air. Instead, it will breathe in birth fluid, if still in the ewe's womb, and you could have a case of pneumonia on your hands.

So to all you moms who have had, or will be having a baby or maybe twins, you've got it made. You're not in a barn; you have trained doctors and nurses, and they know what they are doing!

There was one time when I had a disaster with the sheep. I have worked with over a thousand farmers giving them advice on growing, managing and harvesting many different crops. I know what I am doing. Behind my house and barn there was a field that had brush, small trees and tons of rocks. Using my chain saw I cut the trees down, cleared out the brush and rocks, plowed and prepared the field and planted it to several forage species. One of them was red clover. I knew the dangers of red clover; any ruminant, like sheep or cows, can bloat from eating lush alfalfa or clover. Bloat means gas builds up in the rumen, which is one of the four compartments in the stomach. The other compartments are the reticulum, omasum, and abomasum. By the way, there are a lot of other ruminants that have four stomachs. They include deer, elk, moose, camels, goats and cows to name a few.

To prevent bloat, one needs to feed some hay first, give them time to digest it and only let them out on pasture for maybe ten or fifteen minutes. The first time I let them out to graze this field I followed all these preventative measures. After they had been in the field for ten minutes I went to bring them into the barnyard. As I approached the field, some sheep were already in the barnyard. A few were frothing at the mouth, several staggering and one jumped into the air, landed on her back and died. Now several others were dying. I got the rest of the sheep out of the pasture, locked them in the barnyard and raced to the house. I called the veterinary clinic and told them I had an emergency on my hands. Two veterinarians arrived in ten minutes. Despite their efforts I lost a dozen ewes. I knew what I was doing and I knew all about the potential for bloat. I was puzzled by what happened. I called Cornell's Vet College and they had never heard of such a sudden bloat "attack." I called a researcher I knew from the Agronomy Department who specializes in forage crops. He said Cornell's dairy herd and sheep flock had the exact same thing happen! They lost a lot of animals. Later they found the problem was due to a very unusual weather condition. With unusually warm weather the clover grew abnormally fast and nitrates accumulated rapidly in the tips of the plants. And it is the plant tips that these animals were eating first.

Now a word about farmers: I never considered myself a farmer. But I worked with thousands of them, from the hobby farmer, to the largest farmer in one of the counties I covered, who grew 8,000 acres of corn.

Agriculture is the largest single industry in the world, in the United States, in New York State, in two of the four counties I covered, and in the county I live in. Without the farmer we wouldn't exist. We need to eat. And they supply us with that food. It isn't grown in the grocery store where you shop. Many of the hard working farmers I have known went bankrupt. It is not because they were poor managers. Some were. But most of them buy the inputs they need to produce their crops at retail prices and they sell their crops at wholesale prices. They are at the mercy of the markets and the weather. Please don't complain about the farmer with your mouth full of food.

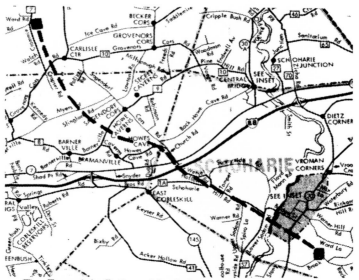

The Tornado's Path — Monday's tornado touched down first on Crommie Road in Carlisle, passed through Howes Cave and along Wetsel Hollow Road and Schoharie Hill Road to Schoharie.

Times Journal Newspaper

CHAPTER 32

THE TORNADO

My job was always full of challenges. Much of it involved counseling with dairy, livestock and cash crop farmers and agricultural business representatives, either on the phone, in the office, or out in the field. Much of my time was spent out in the field. That is why they often referred to me as "the man outstanding in his field."

If I added up the thirty-three years of my career, and looked at my major job responsibilities over that period of time, a high percentage of my job involved four disciplines: dairy science and crop science, which involved about sixty percent of my time, and business management and agricultural engineering, which took up about forty percent of my efforts.

Since only ten percent of the population of the United States are farmers and the other ninety percent are non farm folks, I want to give you a snapshot of what these four disciplines involve.

Dairy science includes dairy herd production, management and marketing, genetics, and animal heath.

Crop science involves forage and grain crop production; management and marketing; establishing research and demonstration trials to find the best crop varieties adaptable to our soil and climatic conditions; weed, disease and insect control; and recommendations and counseling regarding planting, growing and harvesting of forage and grain crops.

Business management includes teaching record keeping and helping clients use those records to analyze their business for rates of crop and animal production, cost control, labor efficiency, and tax management. It also involves partnership arrangements and estate planning.

Agricultural engineering involves the design, remodeling and construction of farm buildings for housing animals, crop storage structures, machinery storage, barn ventilation systems, and manure handling facilities.

It was the latter, agricultural engineering, and specifically barn construction and remodeling, which presented me with one of the most challenging days of my career.

It was a hot, very humid summer day in July 1989. The forecast was for thunderstorms, some possibly severe.

I was in my office and around 2:00 pm. I heard a continuous loud noise outside. It sounded like we were having one of those motorcycle rallies that we have every year right across the street at the County Fairgrounds. I couldn't figure out what it was. So I went outside. It didn't take long to see what was happening.

I have some background in meteorology, having taken a very tough course at Cornell as a student, along with my flight training as a pilot and further training with the National Weather Service as a sky warn observer, where I report severe weather in our county. There were what meteorologists call mammatus clouds in the sky. They were green and purple! These clouds form in very rare instances onto the bottom of cumulonimbus clouds, what we often call thunderheads. The clouds had scalloped bottoms. Some meteorologists refer to them as looking like breasts hanging from the bottoms of the clouds. No kidding.

The continuous flashes of lightning and the deafening roar of thunder was horrifying. I ran into the office and warned everyone, "I think we are in the middle of a tornado!" We were spared but part of Schoharie County was not.

The tornado cut a twelve mile path, hopping and skipping along, from northwest to southeast. Thirty homes were severely damaged or destroyed.

Howe Caverns is a tourist attraction that draws thousands of people from around the country every year. As a matter of fact, spelunkers, those people who are crazy enough to go down into caves, come from around the world to explore our many caves and caverns. One attendant at the Howe Caverns Gift Shop reported that the souvenirs were flying out of shattered windows on one side of the building, while some of those same souvenirs were sucked back into the building from smashed windows on the opposite side of the gift shop!

When I got home that afternoon Karen was crying, she was so scared. She said it was pitch black outside with torrential rain. She ran downstairs and hid behind the couch. I went outside later. We were spared but the tornado was about 1000 feet from our property. I have a small stream with sheep fencing along it. The fence was down and buried under mud and stones from the stream, which overflowed its banks.

But the real challenge came the next morning. When I arrived at the office, I contacted some key officials who could give me an idea of the number of farms that had extensive damage. There were nine. So I set out to see if I could be of any assistance.

I was driving to my first farm but was stopped by a deputy sheriff as I turned into a side road. "You can't go through, sir. The road is impassable with trees across the road and power lines down all over the place." I told him who I was and my intentions and he said, "OK, but it's at your own risk." The power company had several crews there and they had cleared enough of a path for me to get to the first farm, which was about a half mile from Howe Caverns.

When I arrived at the farmstead, the first thing I saw was a large dairy barn with no roof. The farmer came over to me and I said, "Where is the roof?" He pointed and said, "Over there." What was "over there" looked like scores of Christmas trees covered with tinsel. They were large oak trees decorated with sheets of his steel roofing that were dangling from the limbs! Those trees were about one half mile away.

He took me around to show me some of the damage. There was a tractor and a forage wagon parked near the barn. Unfortunately, a wooden stave silo full of silage, which held about four hundred tons of silage, was lying on the ground, split in two. It landed between the tractor and the forage wagon. The farmer had been in the barn while all this was happening. His two sons were up on a hill baling hay. They saw the storm approaching and one son hid under a loaded hay wagon. The other son ran for his pickup truck. He got in but couldn't close the door because the wind was so strong. I got out a set of barn plans and we discussed rebuilding the roof.

The next stop was a similar situation. The dairy stable was damaged but repairable. The farmer's concern was a 20 foot diameter by 50 foot high concrete stave silo that was full of about 500 tons of silage. The top of the silo had been twisted but the steel hoops around the silo held. His concern was how to repair the silo. I called one of our Ag Engineers and he gave me some suggestions on what could be done. I suggested he call the company that constructed the silo.

A third farm was in the beautiful Schoharie Valley. On the way to the farm I made a detour to see if I could follow the tornado's path. It wasn't hard to follow. Some of the largest oak trees around had their upper limbs all twisted up. You could see the counter clockwise twist of the limbs. That twist is from the counterclockwise rotation of the tornado.

By the way, here is an interesting thing that I'll bet you didn't know. If you live in the northern hemisphere, a tornado rotates counter clockwise, as do all low atmospheric pressure systems. That's why I mentioned the tree limbs were twisted in a counterclockwise direction.

If you live in the southern hemisphere the rotation is clockwise. This phenomenon is called the coriolis effect. Do you know why this "effect" happens? It is due to the rotation of the earth. You don't believe me, do you? OK, here's proof. Put the book down and go into the bathroom and flush the toilet. Which way is the water rotating as it goes down the drain? Counter clockwise. Try the same thing in the tub. Fill the tub partially full of water and let the water drain out. Do the same thing in the sink. In all three situations the water spins down the drain counter clockwise. If you were right on the equator, you would not see any effect. I learned all about this when we were in Kenya, Africa.

Sorry for the diversion. When I made the detour to see some of the other damage, I passed a small settlement where there were four mobile homes. I said *were*. Most of what I saw was pink insulation, metal and furniture scattered all around the area.

After my "tour" to assess the damage I drove to the next farm in the valley. The farm had an older barn with a new addition on the south end of it. As I drove in, I was aghast. Where was the new addition? The old barn was unscathed. The farmer said, "the new addition was probably in pieces scattered around in the next county." That wasn't too far from the truth.

The rest of the day was spent visiting the other farmers on my list to see what I could do to help them make decisions on where to go from there. That was not exactly a typical day!

CHAPTER 33

RETIREMENT: GOOD OR BAD?

In 1991, during my last week of work, I sensed that "something" was going on. I thought, I bet the office staff is planning a retirement party. They were. At a staff meeting, the genie was out of the bottle and I said, "If you are planning a retirement party for me, I won't go." "Good," one person said, "We'll have it without you." I thought about that and decided I better show up.

I found out that at the night of the party, there were three other large farm meetings going on involving hundreds of my clients. I thought that was rather poor timing for having my party at the same time many of my clients would be at the other meetings. There probably will be hardly anybody there.

Well, we had a full house. Initially I felt a little uncomfortable. Everyone was shaking my hand wishing me good luck, while I was shaking from the thought that maybe this will be a "roast," where there would be all kinds of stories, some funny, some not so funny and somedown right embarrassing. Many folks stood up to say a few words. But they were all complimentary.

After the dinner I was called up to the podium to receive some gifts. Among them was a gold watch. Why do they always give you a gold watch at retirement? I have two of them and they both work. I listened to it and I told the M.C. "I think you might want to take it back." He said, "You don't like it?" I replied, "It's beautiful, but I'm afraid it's full of ticks" Groan. Groan.

Finally, toward the end of the ceremony, I was asked to say a few words. I introduced the two new Extension Agents who would be replacing me. They both were very tall so I thought I would ham it up a little and do one of my impersonations. I used to be able to do about forty of them. I impersonated Ed Sullivan introducing them as "the reeeely big new Extension Agents who will put on a reeeely big shoe." I should have introduced them as the Bee-els. If you never heard Ed Sullivan talk before then you won't have a clue about what I just wrote.

It was a fun night and of the thousands of meetings I had over my career that will stand out as the best.

Around the time of my retirement party, I received many cards and letters from my friends and clients who congratulated me on my accomplishments and wished me good luck.

Of the many letters I received, one stood out that really touched me. It was from a farmer friend whom I always admired. I do not know of anyone who worked as hard as John did.

After serving his country in the Air Force, he bought a dairy farm in the Schoharie Valley. In addition to milking and caring for his own cows, he also had a milk can route where he picked up a load of milk from many farms early in the morning. At that time, milk from the cows was cooled on the farm in ten gallon milk cans which individually held about 86 pounds of milk. Add the weight of the can and he was handling about 100 pounds each time he lifted a can from the cooler and loaded it on to his truck. He had to handle the heavy cans again when he delivered the truck load of milk to a creamery. Later in the day he picked up the empty cans and delivered them back to the farms.

In the interim, he had to milk his own cows twice a day and do all the other barn chores. He also had to do all the field work from early spring through late fall. This included planting and harvesting all the forage and grain crops to feed to his cows, heifers and calves. This went on for years until the dairy industry shifted to bulk milk tanks on the farm. The milk is now picked up on dairy farms by milk tanker trucks that can hold up to 33 tons of milk on the bigger tankers.

We lost many dairy farmers when the conversion from milk cans to bulk milk tanks occurred. There was a large investment in converting the old milk house or building a new milk house to accommodate this new milk delivery system. In addition, with the weight of the bulk tank trucks, many bridges were condemned because they could not support the weight of the big tanker trucks. This resulted in more farmers being forced out of business. John also had to make the conversion but he stayed in business.

Despite all the hard physical labor, John was always in good spirits and had a sense of humor. On the day of the spring equinox when the days start getting longer he would call me around 5:00 am and say, "Hey Fred, notice the days are getting longer?" He would call me at the fall equinox and ask if I noticed the days were getting shorter.

The title of this book is "Never Say Can't". As you already read, the title came from when my father told me to do something and I would say "I can't". Well. John had nine kids. He would tell them to do something and on occasion they would say, "I can't". John's reply was, "Sell your can't and buy a can". Hey, that could be a title of a book!

I was heart broken when I learned that John died a horrible death from Lou Gehrig's Disease in April 2002. Here is John's letter to me.

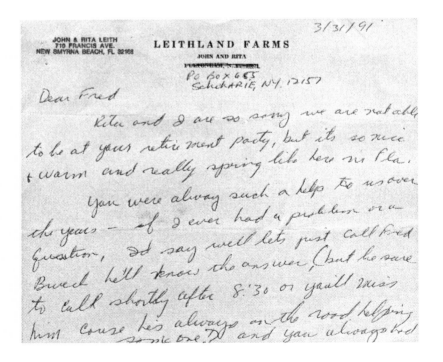

the answer right away or very soon after.
we also remember the farm visits + those
long talks we had full of good advise!

Thanks for everything Fred and best wishes
for a long + happy retirement!

Best wishes
John + Rita Lath

I have known and worked with thousands of people over my thirty-three year career. Much of it was one-on-one, out on the farm, in the office or over the telephone consultations. Over 400 monthly publications were written and sent out to over 1200 farms and ag business people on our mailing list. 1000 radio programs covering several states were broadcast over that time frame. I calculated I had over 3,400 night meetings.

I made scores of friends and still have some contact with these folks.

The day after I retired, it was a bitter sweet experience. It felt like a huge weight had been lifted off my shoulders. At the same time, I felt guilty. No more responsibility in helping people help themselves through Extension educational programs. What do I do now? How about enjoying this new freedom? Now I had more time to spend working in my vegetable and flower gardens, working in the woods, and working on building a new fencing system for my sheep.

So my wife and I, even though we are separated, went on a few more trips. The last trip we took was to Eastern Europe; that included East Germany, Hungary, Poland, Slovakia, the Czech Republic, and Austria. I want to visit with you about some of the highlights.

The ominous Berlin Wall in East Germany was taken down after President Reagen told Gorbachev to "tear down this wall." Today there are only a few reminders of it. There was one short section of the old wall that was still standing, maybe the length of a football field. The wall had murals all along its length that were painted by the people of eastern Berlin.

Dresden was the most heavily bombed city in Germany during World War II. In four days over one hundred thousand people died from Allied bombing raids. Today there is one heavily damaged building left standing as a reminder of the horrors of that war.

There are a lot of Polish jokes. The people of Poland are wonderful to get to know but there are some problems with inefficiency — like waiting three hours on a bus to get across the border into Hungary.

In the city of Warsaw, there was the Old Town Square in a small section of the city that was leveled by bombing raids during World War II. After the war, survivors wanted to rebuild it. But there were no photographs of what each building looked like and people had no recollection of how the buildings looked prior to the war.

Then someone remembered Canaletto's painting of the buildings. So that small city square was reconstructed from that painting.

There were over one hundred different concentration camps scattered throughout Europe during that war. I have been to several on other trips. We were reminded of the unbelievable horror of Hitler's hatred of the Jewish people when we went through some of the buildings of the Auschwitz Concentration Camp.

This was one of the best excursions we ever had. And it was our last! After the horror of September 11th with the terrorist attack in New York City, I feared flying, despite the fact I was a pilot. Karen continues to be a world traveler.

Auschwitz Concentration Camp

CHAPTER 34

ANOTHER CRISIS

In 1996, Karen retired from teaching school. She loved to teach and always said she would teach until she was eighty. (I don't think we have any eighty year old teachers anywhere around here.) She said there were several factors that led her to this decision. There were three kids in school that she was really afraid of. Remember the Oklahoma school shootings? The other thing: she said she would know when it was time. Some people feel you should quit when you're ahead of the game. In any event, she made the big decision.

I don't know how she felt about retiring because we never discussed it. But I know how I felt when I retired. First, I felt like a huge weight was lifted from me. What a relief it was. Now I could do anything I wanted to do and nobody could tell me what to do, or how to do it, or when to do it. Then came the feelings of guilt. I was no longer working with people or helping people make their lives better. But those feelings quickly faded and I got along with my life.

Now for the bad news: It was one of the worst days of my life; I was working outdoors and Karen had gone to town. I went into the house to get a cup of coffee. I noticed there was a message on the answering machine. I pressed the message button and it was our joint attorney. The message said, "Karen I can't make our 1:30 appointment but I'll be free at 4:00 pm." That's strange. She never said anything about seeing our attorney.

Several hours went by and then her car came up the driveway. I was working in the garage at that time. It was rather strange that she sat in the car for over ten minutes. Then I heard the car door close and I went to the edge of the garage to greet her. She had her head down and she was dragging her feet as she slowly walked toward the house. When she got near I said, "Hi." Immediately she started crying hysterically. I asked her, "What's the matter?" No answer. She kept crying. I asked what happened. No answer. What's wrong? No answer. This went on for ten minutes. I put my arm around her and pleaded, "Will you please tell me what is wrong?" She slowly looked up at me and said, "I'm leaving you!" I said, "What?" She repeated it. I couldn't believe what I heard. I asked her what happened, what's wrong, what's going on? Her answer: "It's a matter of lifestyle." She never said anything more about it to me to this day.

She has always been a socialite, a party person, and very outgoing. She has lots of friends and is always going somewhere. She has to be with people. My conclusion? Without her career, she would be stuck home with me and that was unacceptable to her. She had to be out and about. And so we got a legal separation. We are still married. She spends half the year on trips around the world with others. The rest of the time she goes biking, gambling, bowling, goes to the movies or invites over her friends. And so it goes. But surprise, surprise. When she isn't on a trip somewhere in the world, or when she doesn't have a party to go to, she spends the weekend with me at my home. I guess we have the best of both worlds. I can work until I drop, doing what I like to do around my property and she can live her "gypsy" lifestyle. We get along very well; she still is my best friend. But then I don't have that many friends.

Life is a bowl of cherries. But sometimes it's the pits. I believe you have to live your own life. If you can share it with someone else it sure beats living alone. On the other hand, you don't have to keep compromising with someone if you are married or have a live-in friend. To each his own. Life goes on.

using geothermal steam deep within the earth for generating
electricity and heating houses

CHAPTER 35

LANDS OF FIRE AND ICE

You learned earlier that Karen and I separated. But she is still my best friend despite our different lifestyles.

Living alone was difficult but I knew life had to go on and that traveling was part of my life. So that same year I went on a trip to Costa Rica and Karen took care of my sheep!

Costa Rica is a very small tropical country about one third the size of New York State. It is nestled between Nicaragua and Panama in Central America.

Despite its small size, it has, according to our tour guide: 1400 species of trees; 10,000 species of plants, of which 1200 are orchids; ten percent of the world's butterflies, with over 3000 species in one of their National Parks; 35,000 species of insects; 200 species of mammals; 850 species of birds, of which 50 are humming birds; and 200 species of reptiles, half of them snakes. There are twelve tropical life zones in Costa Rica.

Our group was limited to 16 people, so that was a plus in not having to take fifteen minutes boarding a big bus. We all traveled in one big van throughout this travel adventure. And it was an adventure, from two days of horseback riding to white water rafting.

I am not too fond of being in the water because of a near death experience my sister had when she nearly drowned in Lake Ontario. Therefore, I was hesitant to go rafting in category three rapids. I said to myself (here we go again), "I can't do this. I might drown!" But I went anyway. After all, this was a travel adventure!

We had four rafts with four people in each raft. About halfway down the river we entered some rapids and one of the rafts flipped over on top of the people in it. The four people in the raft closest to them jumped in and managed to rescue them. It was a close call; my fear of the water was heightened by this experience.

We spent one day in a tropical rainforest and rode the only aerial tram ride in the world that is located in a rainforest. It took one hour to get to the end and one hour to return. During the ride we were anywhere from six feet above the ground to going over some of the tallest trees. A naturalist accompanied us, explaining all about the habitat around us.

On the way back, clouds darkened and we heard thunder in the distance. Thunderstorms happen every day in Costa Rica, but I wasn't too thrilled about being in a steel cage in a thunderstorm. It wasn't long before we were in a torrential rain for the last ten minutes of the ride. When we finally got back to the starting point, we all ran into a pavilion. Just as the last person got through the door, the pavilion was struck by lightning. There was a bright flash, a deafening bang and the underside of the exposed steel girders on the roof had sparks dancing all along them. Just a few minutes difference and who knows how many of us could have been fried. You learned about what lightning did to my friend, John, in Chapter 5.

The biggest thrill in Costa Rica was our late afternoon arrival and overnight stay at the Arenal Observatory Lodge. This unique lodge doubles as a volcano research station. Here, volcanologists from around the world come to study the volcano. At the time we were there, it was the most active volcano in the world.

arenal volcano

Soon after we arrived we headed for the cafeteria for a late evening supper. Suddenly we heard a huge explosion, the building shook and we ran outside. Just one mile away, the volcano was putting on a show. Smoke, fire, huge rocks, and red hot lava spewed from the open caldera at the top of the mountain. These occurrences continued throughout the night. I was asleep on the bottom of a double bunk bed when an explosion shook the room. I jumped up and smashed my head on the upper bunk, ran outside barefoot with just my undershorts on to watch the fireworks. I have to admit that despite a bad headache, it was worth the experience of being that close to the world's most active volcano.

I learned more about the awesome forces of volcanoes on another trip I took to Iceland in August of 1997. Again, I went alone and joined a group via a local tour company in Albany, New York, which is about forty miles from my home. Karen came over and took care of the sheep again. Now isn't that nice that, although we are separated, we are still friends?

I think there is a lesson to be learned here. Lots of people get divorced and or enter into a separation agreement. I haven't a clue what the statistics are but many wind up bitter enemies. That just makes matters worse. Why not still be friends, even if both couples remarry? It may be awkward but it can make life more peaceful.

Back to Iceland. It is a volcanic island in the Atlantic Ocean near the Arctic Circle. There are no trees because of the harsh climate. The local people joke that if you get lost anywhere in Iceland, just stand up and someone will find you!

To me, the most interesting things about Iceland are the volcanoes, geysers and hot springs which dot the entire country. Over 75 percent of the people heat their homes from the hot springs. Electricity is generated from the steam of those underground springs.

I learned about, and walked on, Vatnojokull Glacier. It is Europe's largest glacier. Underneath it is an accident waiting to happen. Why? There is a volcano underneath the glacier! A number of years ago, the volcano erupted, cutting a hole into the ice. The tremendous heat from the volcano melted the ice. It cut a deep trench into the glacier. A dam was formed. Then, without warning, the hot water broke through the dam, wiping out everything in its path along the flat lands below.

I had an opportunity to go to a horse stable, and ride an Icelandic pony. These ponies are the only horses in the world that have a fifth gait. Horses can walk, trot, canter and pace. The fifth gait is a "running walk" that is so smooth, you don't even bounce. I rode the pony bareback as fast as he could go. You just have to make sure you squeeze your legs tight against the horse's sides. It also helps to know how to ride a horse! It was a fantastic trip.

Speaking of horses, I have to tell you about Rusty. He was our large, very gentle, western quarter horse we had when I lived on the farm as a kid. We had a McClellen U.S. army cavalry saddle, which I have at home now in my recreation room. Sis and I used to ride double. She would be in the saddle and I rode bareback behind her — on the same horse.

When putting a saddle on a horse, some horses resort to an old trick. First you put a horse blanket on the horse's back. Then you put the saddle on top of the blanket. Now here's the trick. Sometimes a horse will take a deep breath and hold it while you are tightening the cinch, which is a leather strap that is connected to one side of the saddle. The strap goes under the horse's belly and around to the other side of the saddle. You tighten the strap and tie it to the saddle. Whenever I saddle a horse I take my knee and forcefully nudge my knee into the horse's belly. This usually makes him exhale so you can tighten the cinch and keep it tight. Why all the fuss? If you don't give him the old knee trick, the saddle can loosen up when he exhales.

So here is what can happen: One day Sis decided to go for a ride with Rusty. Pop, Mom and I were watching as they went down the road. Rusty was running hard, and all of a sudden, Sis and the saddle were under Rusty's belly. We all hollered, "Hang on, Sis." Suddenly Rusty turned around and ran back to the barn, where we caught him. Sis was shook up but uninjured. She could have been dead. She never used the old knee trick.

CHAPTER 36

DANGEROUS OCCUPATIONS

Four of the most dangerous occupations are farming, forestry, fishing and mining.

I am familiar with forestry because I have a small woods that I love to work in. There is only one problem: it's very dangerous. I had a number of friends who were killed cutting down trees. Many farmers have their own wood lot and they have gotten into trouble.

I have had a number of close calls working in my woods. When felling a tree, you can't trust that the tree will fall in the direction you want it to.

The very first thing one needs to do is survey the area. Look overhead. Are there any "widow makers"? These are dead branches on the tree you are cutting or on trees next to the one you are cutting. The branches can come down on you as the tree starts to fall. I know of people who were killed by "widow makers."

Second, one needs to plan an escape route. You never stand by the tree and watch it fall. I did that once and the base of the tree kicked out and missed my legs by about six inches. Get out of the way and run like hell!

Another time I ran in the opposite direction that the tree was falling while cutting down a small tree. I was cutting that tree, and it started to fall in the direction I wanted it to go. Then suddenly it rotated 180 degrees and landed on top of me. I never dropped the chain saw on the ground when I ran. I carried it with me while it was still running. Not a smart thing to do! I landed on top of the saw when the tree landed on me. Luckily I did not have my finger on the "trigger" that makes the chain go around. If I kept my finger on the trigger, with the chain running as the tree pinned me to the ground, I would not be writing this book. I would have been ripped open from my throat to my navel!

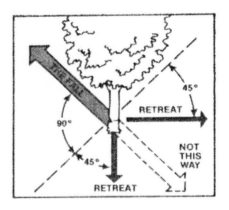

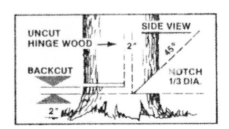

The proper procedure in felling a tree is to clear a path at a 45 degree angle from the direction you want the tree to fall. Then run that way.

In felling a tree, one starts by cutting a notch on the side of the tree in the direction you want it to fall. Then a back cut is made just above where you cut the notch, but on the opposite side of the tree. As you cut into the tree, a hinge is created and, if all goes well, the tree falls where you want it to go. You drop the saw and run like hell. But glance over your shoulder because the tree may be following you! So much for forestry.

Now, on to agriculture, since that is where I have the most expertise.

Farm machinery is a necessity on any farm but it can kill if one becomes careless.

One of the dangers of working with farm machinery is in the use of the power take off (pto) shaft.

I own a 55 horse power tractor. On the back of the tractor is a three point hitch where you can attach many different kinds of implements, from rotary mowers and augers for digging holes to plows, snow blowers and many other implements.

Here is where the danger is. Also on the back of the tractor is a pto or power take off shaft. Any implement that is pto driven can be attached to the back of the tractor. This includes mowers for mowing hay or pastures, rakes for making the hay into windrows, balers for baling the hay into bales, forage choppers to chop corn or hay. And the list goes on.

There are two standard pto speeds: 540 rpm and 1000 rpm. Rpm is revolutions per minute. That means when I attach an implement, like my five foot rotary mower, to the tractor, then attach the mower pto shaft to the tractor, and engage the pto shaft it will revolve 540 times in one minute.

If one stops the tractor, for example, to get or fix something on the other side of the implement you should walk around the back of the implement to get to the other side.

But when in a hurry, there is the temptation to step over the revolving pto shaft to get to the other side. And there is the danger. Catch a pant cuff, a shirt tail that isn't tucked into your belt, a jacket that is open, or any "catchable" piece of clothing, or even make a misstep, and you could be revolving around the shaft 540 or 1000 times per minute! I know of scores of farmers who got caught up in pto shafts. Many died on the spot. Some were lucky and got their pants ripped off. Others lost an arm or a leg. And all for the sake of saving a few seconds by stepping over that rotating shaft. Of course, one can turn off the pto shaft and, for safety's sake, shut off the engine. But they don't think of that.

Another problem, besides the revolving pto shaft, is the implement that the shaft is attached to. Take a forage chopper that is pto driven. As the name implies, it chops up forage into tiny pieces and blows it into a forage wagon that trails behind the chopper. Let's say a slug of hay gets stuck in the throat of the chopper and you reach in to pull it out while the chopper is running. This is an easy way to lose an arm or be pulled into the chopper.

I co-owned an airplane at one time with Cliff, a dairy farmer. We became friends and went on a number of short flights together.

One cold fall day, Cliff had unloaded his last load of corn silage and was sweeping out his self-unloading wagon. The wagon has a chain-in-flight conveyor on the bed of the wagon that slowly moves the load of silage to the front via the tractor pto. In the front of the wagon there are beaters, which rotate in opposite directions. They have long spikes on them that beat up the forage so it flows easier to a cross conveyor in the front of the wagon. The silage is discharged into a forage blower that is pto operated by another tractor and a large fan blows the forage up a pipe that goes to the top of the silo. Today the larger dairy farms have horizontal silos called bunker silos. They are simpler, cheaper and much easier to fill and unload.

Cliff was wearing a pair of coveralls and a leather jacket to stay warm. As he was sweeping the floor, he was backing up as he swept. Suddenly he felt a sharp pain and a tremendous force that was pulling him so tight that he couldn't move. He backed into the rotating beaters! What saved Cliff was his leather jacket and his tremendous strength. He was about six feet five inches and weighed over 230 pounds. He was lucky. I saw the scars on his back one day when we had our shirts off when washing an airplane.

We had a farmer in Montgomery County who was drawn into the beaters and was killed.

There was a farmer I knew who lived four miles from me. He had a self-propelled combine that could pick corn ears off of six rows of corn in one pass through the field. The combine shells the corn off the cob and conveys the grain into a bin on the combine.

He got into an area in the field where there was a lot of weeds in the corn. The weeds jammed the pick-up head of the combine. He reached in, with the combine running, to pull out the weeds. The combine pulled his arm into the machine and he bled to death on the spot.

Once the grain is harvested, it can be put in a storage bin or into a silo. If it goes into a bin it has to be heated and dried down to about fifteen percent moisture for proper storage conditions. I have known farmers who climbed a ladder to check the corn in a bin. They stepped into the bin, stepped into an unstable spot and, like quicksand, they were in over their heads and were suffocated.

Chopped hay or chopped corn can be put into tower silos or horizontal silos as silage. Both types of silos can be dangerous.

A 20 foot diameter by 50 foot tall concrete stave silo can hold around 500 tons of silage. Before feeding the silage, it has to ferment in the silo. It's sort of like fermenting grapes in a wooden barrel, like Pop used to do when making wine.

Under certain conditions, nitrates in the forage can accumulate and form nitrogen dioxide, referred to as silo gas. It is heavier than air and can flow down the silo chute into the barn and kill animals and people. Every fall I sent bulletins to farmers about the dangers of silo gas.

Something that nobody thought about years ago was a silo explosion. The first explosion happened in Pennsylvania. It was in a special sealed silo that is oxygen free. With no oxygen in the silo you can preserve the silage for long periods. Silage has to go through a fermentation process for preservation. In this process, the silage heats up. Sometimes it can get so hot you can have a smoldering silo fire without the flames. In the Pennsylvania case, there was a silo fire in one of these types of silos. The fire department was called. A firefighter climbed up the silo ladder with a fire hose, opened the top hatch of the silo, put the hose down into the silo, turned on the water and BOOM! The top of the silo blew off, killing the fireman. How could this have happened? Remember, this was an oxygen limiting silo. What is H_2O?: two molecules of hydrogen to one molecule of oxygen. Introducing oxygen into the smoldering silage caused the explosion. Who would have thought about that!

Animals can be a problem also. I have a farmer friend from whom I used to buy round bales of hay. On his farm was a grain bin in the upstairs part of the barn. The grain is fed to the cows. To get the grain out of the bin you flip an electric switch and an auger delivers the grain from the bin into a grain cart down below. The grain cart is wheeled around the barn, dispensing grain to the animals. Guess what! One morning Carl, and his son, Mark, went into the barn and the grain in the bin had been emptied onto the barn floor downstairs. What happened? During the night, a raccoon climbed the stairs to get to the grain and accidentally turned on the switch to the auger. Who would have thought of that happening!

Yes, farming can be dangerous and sometimes strange things do happen. It takes a lot of hard work, sometimes using dangerous machinery, huge investments with very little return on their money, for farmers to produce what we take for granted.

And while we are talking about the dangers of farming, homeowners have dangerous equipment also. People have been hurt by rotary lawnmowers. How about that roto-tiller you use to prepare the soil for your garden? Or your snow blower used to clean your driveway? These are power driven implements, a lot smaller than farm equipment, but nonetheless, they can be very dangerous. Have you ever read the instruction manual when you purchased a piece of equipment? Best to do so. It could save you from trouble!

Here are a few thoughts about getting yourself into trouble when operating any hazardous piece of equipment. It could be a power saw or drill, lawn mower, electric hedge trimmer, garden roto-tiller, snow blower, kitchen electric appliances, like a can opener, cake mixer, electric knife, garbage disposal.

Here are a few examples of some no-no's that could get you into trouble. You can think of a lot more.

Don't read the instruction manual.

Don't heed the warning label on the equipment you are operating.

Don't wear eye goggles when using a grinding wheel or any equipment that can cause pieces of metal or wood to get into your eye.

Don't shut off your snow blower when you try to unclog snow lodged in throat of the blower or in the discharge chute.

Do use your hand to force kitchen garbage or waste into the kitchen garbage disposal

Do let your young child sit with you when operating your riding lawn mower

Do overload your Christmas tree with lots of lights

Do forget to add water daily to your Christmas tree stand

Remember the slogan, "the life you save may be your own."

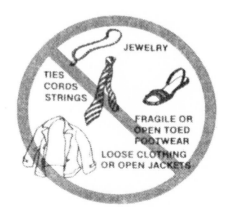

CHAPTER 37

LIFE GOES ON

Now that I am living alone and reflect on my situation, there are times of loneliness. Then there is the fact that I am basically alone in this world. As you learned, I am married but separated. I have no grandparents, no parents, no sisters or brothers, no children and obviously no grandchildren.

So what does one do in this kind of a situation? This was not a hard decision for me to make. The first thing is to have a positive attitude. One could use the "I can't" words and say, "I can't go on like this" or "I have no life and I can't go out because there's nobody to go out with." The excuses can go on but that doesn't solve the problem.

The answer for me was to carry on a legacy of helping others. When professionally employed, I was helping others help themselves through educational programs in my professional career.

Now I am continuing to help people by my involvement with charitable organizations. You could do the same. It could be as simple as sending a check in the mail, which I have done for years, or becoming a volunteer.

How about becoming a member of a Board of Directors of a charitable organization. What about gifting some charitable organization through your will? No taxes involved there.

I am currently doing all of the above. Several years ago, I became a volunteer for the American Red Cross of Northeastern New York, which serves eight countries. A short time later, I became a member of our local county Red Cross Advisory Board and soon became a director for the eight county Northeastern New York Chapter of the American Red Cross.

By doing so, I am with other people, not just in a social way, but in a helping way. It's a great feeling to know you are helping someone or perhaps scores of people who are in need.

No one knows what lies ahead. We can't predict the future. But I do know that when I pass on, having rewritten my will, ten different charitable organizations, each having a separate mission, will have been gifted by my estate. And it will all be non-taxable!

With my attorney, I wrote up a contract for each charitable organization. The gifted organizations are restricted to programs helping people. Nothing can be used for capital expenditures, such as buying office equipment, adding on to, or remodeling offices or buildings. These gifts will also be restricted to the county I live in. Why? I feel I will be getting "more bang for the buck" by having the money spent for local people in need. One can gift regional, state or national charitable organizations but then you have much less control over how you wanted your gift to be spent.

It's people helping people. Hey, that's what I did for thirty three years. Now, that will continue after I pass on. What a great feeling!

How about you? What are your plans for the future? Do you have a will? Is it up to date? Do you have an estate plan? Many people keep putting these important things off. Why? Perhaps they can't face the fact that sometime they will pass on. Tomorrow's another day. That day may never come. And for heaven's sake please don't use the "I can't" excuses. You can, you should and you will do the right thing.

CHAPTER 38

THE FINAL WORD

The goal of my visit with you via this book has been to tell you a factual story about the life and times, the disappointments and failures, but also the victories and successes, of one person.

What you make of your life is up to you. It is what you do with your life that counts.

Look again at the title of this book. What does it say? You may not remember its contents, but I hope you got the message.

Don't feel sorry for yourself because of life's problems and disappointments. Be the best that you can be. If you fall down, you have to get yourself back up. If you fail in something you have to start over again. We all have our problems to deal with. Try to turn problems into opportunities. And never say, "I can't."

Thank you for letting me share my story with you and God Bless.

ABOUT THE AUTHOR

The author, now retired, has a BS degree from Cornell University and a Masters degree from Colorado State University. He has received ten Distinguished Service Awards for excellence in teaching, writing, and carrying out educational programs over his professional career of thirty three years. He has a truly unique writing style where he is communicating specifically with you throughout this book. It is a one on one dialogue with you. Over his career he has worked with over two thousand clients in counseling, recommending, and teaching them to be the best they can be. You will be the recipient of his vast knowledge as you read through the chapters.

Printed in the United States
15668LVS00005B/232-255